ChatGPT Demystified

ChatGPT Demystified

Transform Your World with The Power Of AI

Harish Pursnani

ChatGPT Demystified

This title is available in Paperback, Hard Cover and as an eBook.

The publisher publishes in a variety of print and electronic formats and by print-on-demand. Some material included with standard print versions of this book, may not be included in e-books or in print-on-demand.

First edition, 2023

To the audacious thinkers and bold doers who defy convention and dare to dream, this book is dedicated to you. Your courage to pursue the unconventional is a beacon for innovation and progress. In your pursuit of extraordinary ideas, may this book serve as a valuable tool.

Contents

Foreword

Amidst the evolving landscape of Artificial Intelligence (AI), few innovations have captivated the imagination like ChatGPT. This book serves as your comprehensive guide to understanding and harnessing the power of this transformative technology. My aim is to demystify ChatGPT, making it accessible to everyone, irrespective of their technical background.

ChatGPT is not just a technological revolution, but a lifestyle revolution. Embracing this AI can unlock a wealth of time, allowing you to spend precious moments with loved ones, pursue hobbies, and even kickstart new businesses. Instead of fearing this technology, I encourage you to embrace it. Through this book, I aim to guide you on how to tap into this revolution.

With ChatGPT at your disposal, you can achieve more, faster. The dream of becoming a millionaire is now within closer reach.

Who is this book for?

This book is written with one overarching goal: to empower any reader, regardless of their background or level of education, to unlock the transformative power of AI through ChatGPT. It is an educational tool suitable for both beginners and those seeking more structured knowledge and practical examples.

My goal is to provide clarity for all readers, empowering them to confidently engage in AI-related discussions. This book aims to equip you with knowledge that safeguards against attempts at mystification or power play, thereby democratizing the AI conversation. By demystifying jargon, my goal is to create an environment where everyone, regardless of their background, can participate meaningfully in discussions about AI and its fascinating applications.

This book is an accessible and comprehensive guide intended for anyone keen to understand and utilize the power of ChatGPT. It is suitable for beginners curious about AI, students, educators, entrepreneurs, professionals in any field, and AI enthusiasts. It breaks down complex concepts into digestible content for beginners while providing depth for the experienced.

With a clear, jargon-free approach, this book will guide you on how to harness ChatGPT's potential to enhance and redefine productivity. It is your key to a new world of limitless possibilities, where complex tasks become simpler and goals become more attainable.

What does the book cover?

The possibilities with ChatGPT are infinite, and this book just scratches the surface. The intent is to educate as many people as possible in simple terms and open the door to integrating AI in all aspects of life.

This book is organized into three main sections and a conclusion section with a comprehensive glossary, and a quiz.

Section 1 lays the foundation of your AI journey with ChatGPT. The chapters here introduce basic concepts, principles, and mechanics, setting the stage for the detailed exploration and nuanced understanding of ChatGPT that unfolds later in the book. Thoroughly grasping the chapters in this Section will equip you with the foundational knowledge needed to appreciate the possibilities of AI in the context of ChatGPT as we explore more topics. **I strongly recommend dedicating time to understand the material presented in Section 1 before exploring the rest of the book**.

Section 2 explores ChatGPT's applications in everyday life. Whether you are writing product descriptions, generating creative content, planning events, launching your dream business, or exploring interactive storytelling, this section provides you guidance with numerous examples on leveraging ChatGPT's capabilities in various personal and professional aspects of life.

Section 3 covers advanced topics, further demystifying the technology and starting you on a broader journey. While I have made efforts to make this book accessible to a wide audience, the power of ChatGPT can be unleashed infinitely with an understanding of how to integrate it with other applications, computer programs, and the Web – topics that are covered in this section.

A comprehensive Glossary section facilitates a better understanding of AI concepts and related terminology.

To supplement your learning, the Quiz section at the end is designed to test and reinforce your understanding of the material. Taking the quiz will help you grasp key concepts and can greatly enhance your learning.

Important Considerations

While every effort has been made to ensure the accuracy and usefulness of the information in this book, please bear a few things in mind.

This book is intended to be educational, and you are ultimately responsible for any outcomes that may result from using the information contained within.

This book is based on information available at the time of its publication, July 2023.

As you read this book, you will notice that I have involved ChatGPT in several parts of the book. I used ChatGPT for most of the conversational real-world examples I have included. The exact phrasing for you might vary as ChatGPT generates responses differently each time. When needed, occasionally, I used it to refine or clarify parts of the content I drafted.

AI, including ChatGPT, is a powerful tool but not infallible. Language Models[1] like ChatGPT can sometimes generate inaccurate or false information, known as 'hallucinations.' Therefore, always double-check facts during your interactions with ChatGPT. Avoid making critical decisions solely based on ChatGPT's responses, and seek expert advice when necessary.

Lastly, bear in mind that the world of AI is constantly evolving. While I have made efforts to provide up-to-date information at the time of writing, new developments and improvements are always on the horizon. So, stay curious, continue learning, and keep exploring the fascinating world of AI.

Welcome to the AI Revolution

The future is here, and it is more exciting than ever. Welcome to your voyage into the future with AI and ChatGPT!

[1] I will explain what a language model is in the Introduction Chapter

SECTION 1: Understanding ChatGPT

Everything you need to know to become proficient today

1. Introduction

A. What is ChatGPT?

ChatGPT, at its core, is a computer program that has been designed to communicate and interact much like humans do. Its potency and efficacy come from its extensive 'training' on substantial volumes of curated data sourced from the internet.

Developed by OpenAI[2], ChatGPT is an AI language model that can be considered as a type of a computer program. It's a complex one that uses algorithms and mathematical models to process and generate text. However, unlike traditional computer programs that follow explicit instructions written by programmers, an AI language model learns patterns from data and makes predictions based on those patterns. It is based on GPT, or Generative Pre-trained Transformer, architecture. As its name implies, it is a *pre-trained* model

[2] OpenAI is an American artificial intelligence (AI) research laboratory and corporation. OpenAI conducts AI research with the declared intention of promoting and developing friendly AI. For more information, please visit en.wikipedia.org/wiki/OpenAI or openai.com.

designed to *generate* human-like text. More about *transformer* in the next section B.

ChatGPT's 'learning[3]' process relies on a scientific method known as supervised machine learning. In supervised learning, an AI model is trained on a large set of data that is already labeled with the correct answers. This approach can be likened to how a student learns under the watchful eye of a teacher.

For ChatGPT, the training involves an extensive array of text data in multiple languages culled from the internet. This broad training base enables it to pick up patterns, facts, and even elements of reasoning contained within the data. This also enables it to interact in languages other than English although its performance can vary.

However, it is important to note that the model does not possess consciousness or understanding of the text as humans do. Instead, to re-iterate, it identifies patterns from its training and uses them to generate responses. In essence, it is predicting what comes next in a sequence based on patterns it learned during training. Although it has learned from a diverse range of data, ChatGPT does not hold (a memory of)

[3] The 'learning/training' process involves adjusting internal parameters based on the data a model is trained on, which in the case of language models is usually a vast amount of text. After the training phase, the model can generate text, answer questions, summarize text, and perform various other language-related tasks.

specifics about which documents were part of its training set, nor can it access any particular original source.

From here—post-training, these models do not have direct access to or store specific documents, books, or sources of information. Nonetheless, there are ways to infuse more specific or private data into their knowledge. These primarily include fine-tuning or integration with other computer programs, or via plugins (add-on programs). These topics are quite technical, but I will briefly touch upon them in Section 3 on advanced topics.

Over time, OpenAI has released several versions of ChatGPT, each iteration an enhancement on the previous. The most recent version, ChatGPT 4, is designed to excel specifically in tasks involving natural language understanding and generation.

At the time of this book's publication, there have been strides toward extending ChatGPT's capabilities using plugins, which are software add-ons. These plugins, mostly from vetted third parties, can interact with the web, other forms of data, and different software programs, thereby diversifying the powerful ways in which ChatGPT can be employed. OpenAI has released these capabilities primarily for their paid version of ChatGPT, called ChatGPT Plus.

Apart from Section 3 on advanced topics, this book is based on the free version of ChatGPT

B. How does ChatGPT work?

At its core, ChatGPT uses a large neural network[4] called a Transformer. This neural network is trained on vast amounts of text data, enabling it to learn patterns, grammar, facts, and even some reasoning abilities.

ChatGPT processes text in chunks known as tokens. These tokens can be as short as one character or as long as one word. The model reads these tokens and generates new ones based on the patterns it has learned during training.

A key strength of ChatGPT is its ability to handle context. As it processes tokens, it keeps track of the context and relationships between words and phrases. This ability enables it to generate coherent and contextually relevant responses.

However, while ChatGPT is a remarkable artificial intelligence tool, it is important to acknowledge that it is not flawless. For example, a significant limitation is its inability to access real-time information or retrieve up-to-date knowledge beyond its training cut-off date (except when ChatGPT is integrated with the Web or with another program that enables it to access current information.). So, on its own

---

[4] A neural network is a system or a model used in computers that is designed to work like the human brain. Just like our brain has billions of neurons that help us think, learn, and make decisions, a neural network has many interconnected parts called "nodes" or "neurons" that process information and learn from it. This learning (generally of prediction of patterns and next words based on highest probability) allows the computer to recognize patterns, make decisions, and solve problems, just like we do!

it cannot provide the latest news updates, stock market prices, or any other dynamic data that changes in real-time.

Another limitation is its potential to generate responses that, while grammatically correct and contextually fitting, might not always be factually accurate or sensible. At times, it might even produce creative but misleading interpretations of your prompts. As we continue in the book, we will learn how to interact effectively with ChatGPT while being aware of its limitations.

It is essential to understand these limitations to appropriately set expectations when interacting with ChatGPT, and to verify any critical information it provides, especially in high precision fields such as medical or legal advice.

Despite these limitations, the power of ChatGPT is undeniable, and its potential is immense. It still represents a significant advancement in the field of AI. And, OpenAI continues to make improvements to it regularly. ChatGPT's ability to understand and respond in a way that is contextually appropriate, its new capabilities to connect with the live web and other programs through plugins, and its availability on mobile devices, make it a powerful tool for an almost infinite number of applications – from writing assistance, creative content generation, programming help, learning new topics, language translation, research, to finance, and even for music and art.

Now that you have a better understanding of what ChatGPT is, how it works, and some of its strengths and limitations, we can move onto the exciting parts - using it!

In the forthcoming chapters, you will learn how to interact with ChatGPT, understand its interface and functionalities, how to direct the conversation, give instructions, use system messages, and manage the output.

I hope that this exploration has piqued your curiosity and fueled your excitement. So, fasten your seat belts and get ready to dive into the fascinating world of interacting with AI.

Let the adventure begin!

2. Getting Started

In this chapter, we will explore the necessary steps to get started with ChatGPT. From accessing it to understanding its basic commands, you will gain the knowledge needed to utilize its potential effectively.

A. Access

The first step is to familiarize yourself with how to access ChatGPT. It is as straightforward as visiting the OpenAI website **https://openai.com/**, creating an account, and voilà, you are all set to harness the power of ChatGPT!

Once you are logged in, ChatGPT can be accessed directly at **https://chat.openai.com/**

For a more interactive experience and additional benefits, you might want to consider opting for the latest version of ChatGPT called ChatGPT Plus, available for a nominal monthly subscription fee.

For free access, OpenAI does limit system usage. You can view this allocation and your usage at

https://platform.openai.com/account/usage

Currently, the limit is quite generous and should suffice for most typical users. Of course, this could change at any time, subject to OpenAI's terms.

Note that due to high demand, usage of ChatGPT, particularly the latest version, may occasionally be limited even for paying users. Typically, this limitation lasts for an hour.

B. Engaging with ChatGPT

There are several ways you can engage with ChatGPT:

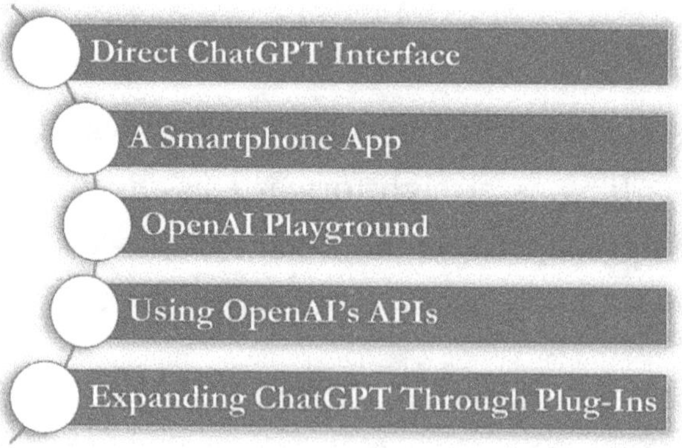

Figure 2-1 Ways to Engage with ChatGPT

1. Direct ChatGPT Interface

The Direct ChatGPT Interface is your primary route to experiencing ChatGPT. This interface provides a focused setting for conversational interactions, making it an excellent tool for tasks that require immediate dialogue or brainstorming.

Access this interface by visiting the OpenAI website (**https://chat.openai.com**) and logging into your account.

This interface, where you interact with ChatGPT through a textbox, is as straightforward as it gets.

We will explore this interface in more detail in its own dedicated chapter in this section.

NOTE: In the spirit of the scope of the book, examples in this book assume using Direct ChatGPT interface unless otherwise noted.

Going forward in this book, I will refer to this interface simply as ChatGPT interface unless I have to differentiate it due to context.

2. A Smartphone App

The Official OpenAI Smartphone app for ChatGPT means you can carry the power of ChatGPT wherever you go. At the time of writing this book, it is available for iOS, and according to OpenAI, it is coming soon for Android users. This app mimics the basic Direct ChatGPT interface in functionality, allowing seamless interaction with ChatGPT on-the-go. If you log in with the same username across your devices, you can access your interaction history at any time.

3. OpenAI Playground

The OpenAI Playground serves as an expansive testing ground where you can not only interact with ChatGPT but also experiment with and adjust factors that significantly affect its responses. It is a user-friendly platform, but you might need some practice before you can fully harness its potential.

Access this interface by visiting the OpenAI website (**https://platform.openai.com/playground**) and logging into your account.

We will explore this interface in more detail in its own dedicated chapter in this section.

4. Using OpenAI's APIs (Application Programming Interfaces)

Application Programming Interfaces (APIs) are a set of rules and protocols that allow software applications to communicate with each other. APIs define how different software components should interact and exchange data, acting as a bridge between different software systems. APIs make it possible for the features or data of one application to be used in another, enabling greater functionality and interoperability.

OpenAI has published standard APIs to embed ChatGPT's capabilities within your existing computer programs, greatly expanding its use cases. Practically all of the capabilities that users use in the interfaces described above and many more advanced capabilities are available.

This topic is somewhat complex for the scope of this book but I will touch upon it in a dedicated chapter in Section 3.

5. Expanding ChatGPT Through Plugins

A plugin can be described as a software component that adds a specific feature or functionality to an existing application. In the case of ChatGPT, plugins offer ways to extend and diversify the capabilities of the language model.

Plugins are an exciting addition to ChatGPT. Initially, the roll-out of plugins is confined to a select group of ChatGPT Plus users. OpenAI aims to gradually increase access as they gain more insights into their utilization. This will eventually extend to API users who wish to integrate these plugins into their own products.

Plugin developers, can build a plugin for ChatGPT. Once constructed, the plugin is listed in the prompt displayed to the language model, accompanied by guidance on its use.

The first series of plugins have been devised by various contributors, including Expedia, Instacart, Kayak, Klarna, Milo, OpenTable, Shopify, Slack, Speak, Wolfram, Zapier etc. These initial plugins mark a key milestone in the ongoing development of ChatGPT and its interaction paradigm with human users.

Similar to APIs, this topic is somewhat advanced for the scope of this book and I will touch upon it in a dedicated chapter in Section 3.

C. Usage Limits

OpenAI has implemented usage limits for interactions (API calls[5] to) with its models. These limits apply to all types of engagement methods e.g., the Direct ChatGPT interface, smart phone app, the Playground Interface or via APIs. In case of usage via the Playground or APIs, the cost varies based on the model chosen. These usage limits are put in place to ensure fair access for all users, to manage the load on the system, and to control costs.

The "usage" in "usage limit" refers to the computational resources consumed when you send a prompt to the model and get a response. This round-trip interaction is also known as "Completion". This can be influenced by factors such as the length and complexity of the prompts and responses, and the number of prompts you send.

Here is how it typically works:

- Each API call to/interaction with the model consumes some number of "tokens".
- *Both* your prompt and the model's response are broken down into these tokens, and

[5] All interactions with ChatGPT (for example, using the interfaces described in this chapter) are converted to API calls in the background.

- The *total* number of tokens affects how much of your usage limit is consumed.

For instance, if your usage limit is 1000 tokens and you make an API call that uses 50 tokens, you would then have 950 tokens remaining.

Tokens are not directly correlated to a simple count of words or characters, as different words and phrases can require different numbers of tokens.

However, the specifics around usage limits, including how they are calculated and enforced, could vary and may be updated by OpenAI anytime. Please check OpenAI's current documentation to get the most accurate and up-to-date information on usage as well as costs.

The usage time of ChatGPT for a user can be affected by a number of factors, most notably the length and complexity of the inputs and outputs.

Here are some examples of how usage time might be affected:

1. **Short, simple exchanges**: If you are engaging in very short and straightforward exchanges with ChatGPT, the usage time will be very minimal. For instance, if you ask "What is the capital of Japan?", the model generates a response in seconds, counting towards the usage time.
2. **Long, complex exchanges**: If you are asking more complex questions or engage in a longer conversation, this

will increase usage time. For example, if you ask the model to generate a summary of a complex scientific article, it will need more time to generate a detailed and accurate summary, which will count towards the usage time.

3. **Sequential conversations**: If you are having an ongoing conversation with the model over an extended period of time, the usage time will continue to accumulate. Each *prompt + response* interaction contributes to the total usage time.

4. **Bulk requests**: If you submit a bulk request to generate responses to a large number of prompts at once, this will also significantly increase usage time. For example, if a company is using ChatGPT to generate responses to customer inquiries and submits hundreds of prompts at once, the time it takes to generate all of these responses will count towards the usage time.

Please note that idle time, or time spent not interacting with the model, does not count towards the usage limit. Only the time taken by the model to generate responses counts towards this limit.

D. Summary

In summary, this chapter is your basic essential guide to initiating your journey with ChatGPT. We walked through the process of accessing ChatGPT via OpenAI's website and explored the various methods to engage with ChatGPT.

The Direct ChatGPT Interface whether on the web or on your smartphone is essentially all you need to get started. If you want to experiment and learn the intricacies, the OpenAI Playground will be key. OpenAI's APIs present an opportunity to integrate ChatGPT's functionalities within your existing software or applications. Furthermore, the scope of ChatGPT can be expanded with the use of plugins, which are new additions designed to extend the model's capabilities.

Varying usage limits are imposed on interactions with ChatGPT. By understanding these limits and how different types of engagements affect them, you will be equipped to navigate ChatGPT effectively.

With this knowledge, we have set a solid foundation for your ChatGPT journey. Now let's dive deeper into the ChatGPT Interface and OpenAI Playground.

3. Navigating the ChatGPT Interface

The ChatGPT interface simplifies the user experience and encourages engagement. For instance, consider the example where you need to brainstorm for a new project idea. You would initiate the conversation by typing, "Generate some innovative ideas for a renewable energy project.". ChatGPT responds by generating a list of possible project ideas, each one detailed and thought-provoking, ultimately helping you progress your brainstorming process. This back-and-forth exchange mimics a real-time conversation, making the Direct ChatGPT Interface a preferred choice for many users.

Effective usage of ChatGPT comes with understanding prompts – a set of text instructions that guide the AI's response. For example, if you want ChatGPT to help draft an email, you could start with a prompt like 'Compose an email to my boss about requesting a day off.'. Clear and specific prompts yield more accurate and relevant responses.

We will explore the techniques of writing effective prompts (also known as Prompt Design or Prompt Engineering) in a dedicated chapter in this section.

A. The ChatGPT Interface

Below is a description of the features of the ChatGPT interface. These features are designed to be extremely simple to get used to quickly.

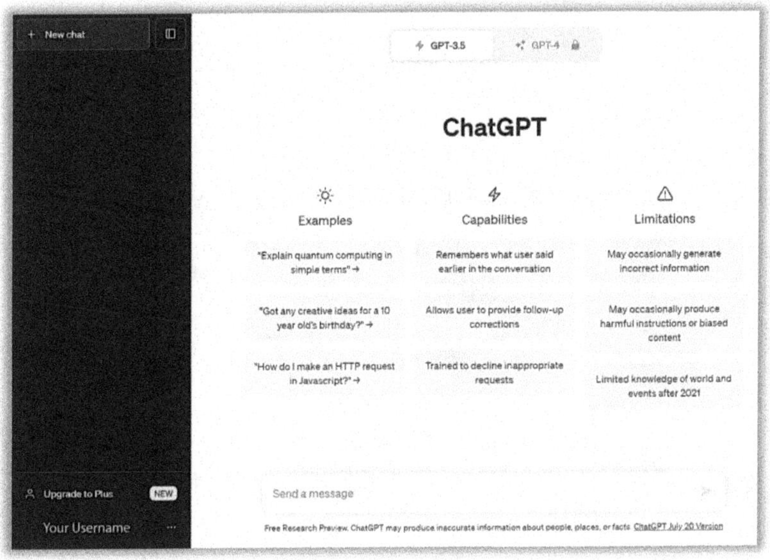

Figure 3-1 ChatGPT Interface

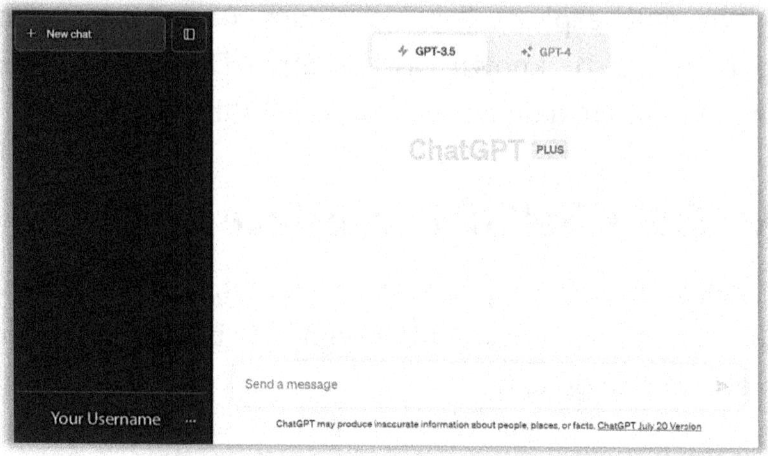

Figure 3-2 ChatGPT Plus Interface (Paid Version)

1. **Prompt Input Area**: This is the text box where you type your instructions, questions, or conversation starters to interact with ChatGPT.

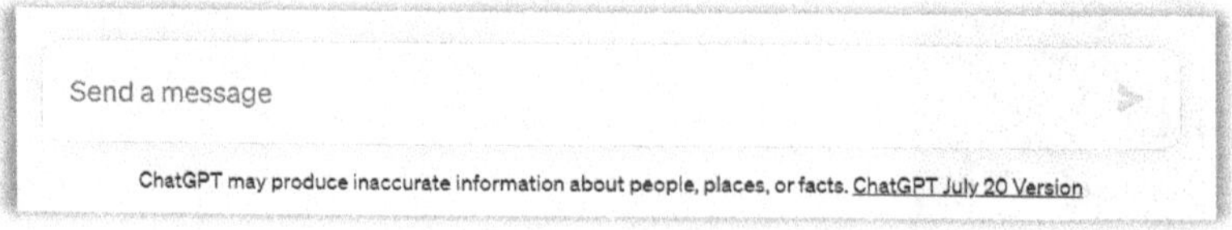

2. **Send Button**: After typing your message in the input field, you click this to send your message to ChatGPT for processing.

3. **Response Area**: This is the section which occupies most of the screen and where responses from ChatGPT appear. It will typically indicate that the message is from "ChatGPT". For paying users, it displays "ChatGPT Plus" (see Figure 3-2).

Here, when you first log in, you can also access Examples and Read a summary of ChatGPT's capabilities and limitations (see Figure 3-1).

4. Each response from ChatGPT is displayed together with icons that provide you the ability to

   i. copy AI responses. 

   ii. provide feedback on the responses generated. 

5. **Chat History**: This area is the column on the left of the screen and it displays all the sessions of back-and-forth messages between you and ChatGPT. In this section, you are able to

   i. Hide or Show the Chat History side bar. 

   ii. Start a new chat. 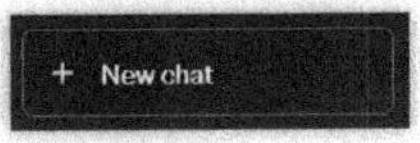

   iii. Delete an old chat. 

   iv. Share a link to your chat. 

   v. Rename a chat session per your needs so you can easily recall the topic of the chat. 

   vi. Upgrade to a paid subscription of ChatGPT Plus

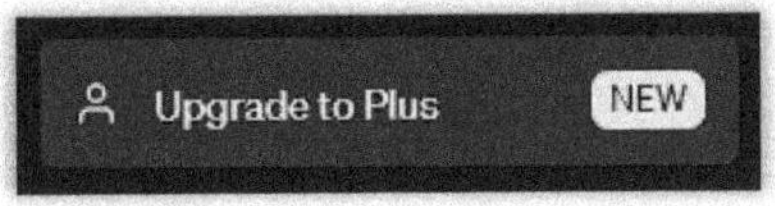

vii. Access **Help & FAQ**, Access **User Settings** and **Log out**, by clicking on the ellipsis next to your username at the bottom of the Chat History.

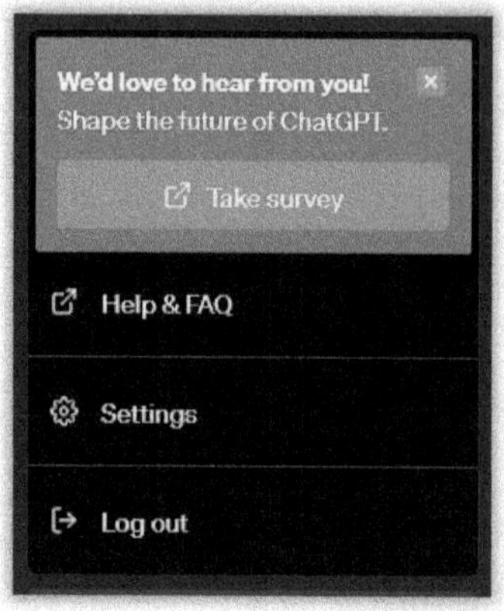

Please note that, by default, all chats are stored by OpenAI to further train ChatGPT.

6. **User Settings**: OpenAI provides simple control of your interface and data through User Settings. You can:

i. In the General Section:

- Change the Theme/look of your interface between Light and Dark
- Clear all your chats

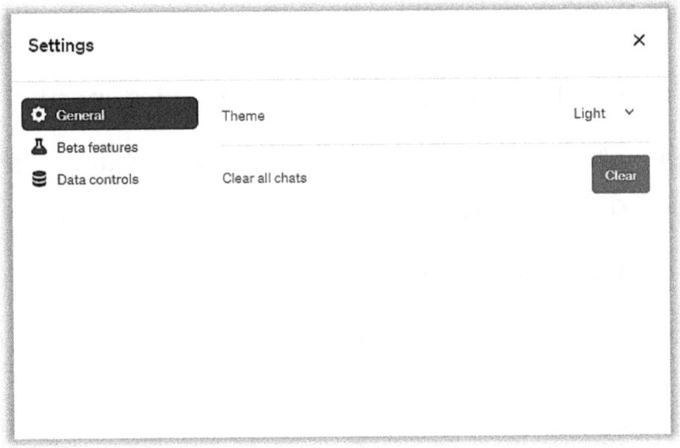

Figure 3-3 ChatGPT User Settings - General Section

ii. If you are a ChatGPT Plus user, you can enable or disable Beta features like Web Browsing and Plugins for ChatGPT. Options enabled here become available for your chats with ChatGPT.

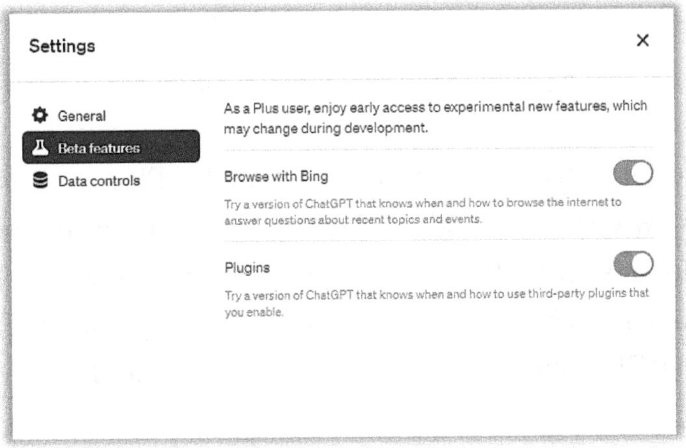

Figure 3-4 ChatGPT User Settings - Beta Features Section

iii. In the Data controls section:

- Disable saving of your chats (device specific)
- Manage the Shared Links to your chats – view and delete them
- Export data for all your chats
- Delete your OpenAI account

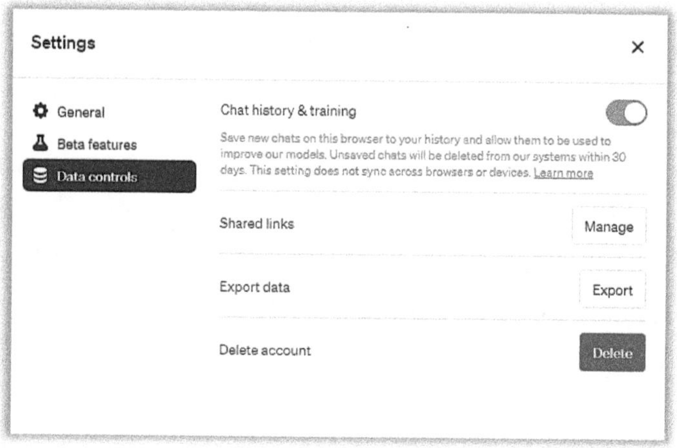

Figure 3-5 ChatGPT User Settings - Data Controls

7. **Model Selector**: If you are a ChatGPT Plus customer, for a new chat, the model selector on the top of the interface allows you to select between different versions of GPT, like GPT-3.5 or GPT-4. This feature is not available on the ChatGPT phone app at the time of writing of this book.

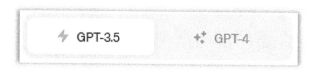

Also available exclusively to ChatGPT Plus users, if you select GPT-4 (or the latest model available), you can use the advanced/beta features that you enabled in settings earlier like extending ChatGPT with Web browsing capabilities and with plugins.

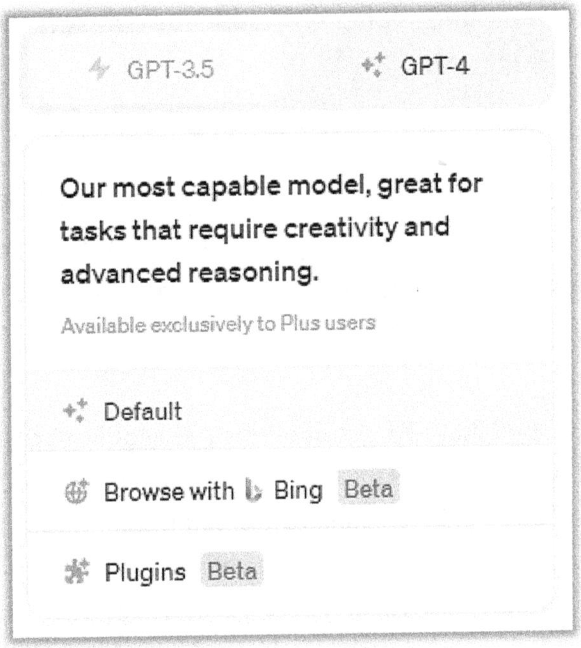

Figure 3-6 ChatGPT Plus - Advanced Features

As this book was published, GPT-3.5 was set to retire, with GPT-4, previously exclusive to paying customers, becoming the default. It is likely that future models, like GPT-5, will first be accessible to ChatGPT Plus users.

B. Summary

In summary, this chapter gives you a complete understanding of the ChatGPT interface. We broke down the interface into its components: including chat history for managing your interactions. User settings offer control over your interface and data, with additional beta features for ChatGPT Plus users.

The model selector for ChatGPT Plus users allows the selection of different versions of GPT. With this knowledge, you are now ready to navigate the ChatGPT Interface and start interacting with ChatGPT effectively.

NOTE: The ChatGPT Interface or the Mobile App is often the perfect fit for most users, offering a straightforward way to interact with ChatGPT. Feel free to skip the next chapter on the OpenAI Playground which is somewhat technical.

However, for those seeking for deeper insights and to build expertise, the OpenAI Playground provides a fascinating sandbox to experiment with and fine-tune ChatGPT's responses. It is like getting under the hood of your favorite car - a bit more complex, but rewarding. In essence, it is your stepping stone to mastering the intricacies of ChatGPT.

This knowledge of a deeper understanding of ChatGPT could even pave the way to new job or business opportunities!

4. Navigating OpenAI Playground: A Lab for ChatGPT

The OpenAI Playground is a platform for experimenting with ChatGPT. It enables diverse prompts, fine-tuning of AI responses, and exploration of different AI models. Each model has unique capabilities, with some being better suited for tasks like translations or speed. Although the in-depth explanation of each model isn't within this scope, you can obtain a brief overview by hovering over them in the Playground interface or visiting the OpenAI website.

ChatGPT, a version of the "text-davinci" model fine-tuned for conversation, is the primary AI used in the Direct Chat Interface. It's derived from the Generative Pretrained Transformer (GPT) model.

When interacting with ChatGPT in the Playground, you have the liberty to adjust settings and parameters, influencing

ChatGPT's creativity, randomness, and response length. This flexibility allows for customization and fine-tuning of responses to cater to specific needs.

Contrastingly, in the Direct Chat Interface, these settings are hidden and optimized for general conversation. You just type your prompts and get responses. Therefore, while the Playground offers more control and application range, it necessitates a better understanding for effective usage.

Below is the summary of some key differences between the Direct ChatGPT Interface and OpenAI Playground.

	Direct ChatGPT Interface	OpenAI Playground
Purpose	Simplified conversational experience	Detailed experimentation and model testing
Best Suited For	Most users.	Users who need more control.
Capabilities	Single model Chat	Access to multiple ChatGPT AI models
Weaknesses	Limited customization of AI behavior	Can be complex for beginners
Best Practices	Use clear, specific prompts, provide necessary context	Experiment with different models and settings, test varying prompts

A. The OpenAI Playground Interface

The Playground interface is divided into two sections with some common elements on the top and bottom of these two sections.

- The left section which covers most of the screen is where you interact with the ChatGPT Model.
- The section on the right is a panel where you select the type of interaction, the Model you want to interact with and the parameter settings to change its behavior.

The section on the left as well as the parameter settings available on the right change based on the first setting "Mode" i.e., the type of interaction you select on the right-hand side (see Figure 4-2).

Select the mode that aligns with your needs best. Here is an overview of the modes available followed by detailed explanations.

1) **Complete Mode**: for interaction with ChatGPT with all parameters possible to calibrate response from ChatGPT

2) **Chat Mode**: for simpler chat interaction with ChatGPT. This mode allows to set an overall context for the chat session (see details below in the "Chat Mode" section.

3) **Edit Mode**: where you can provide a text that needs editing according to instructions.

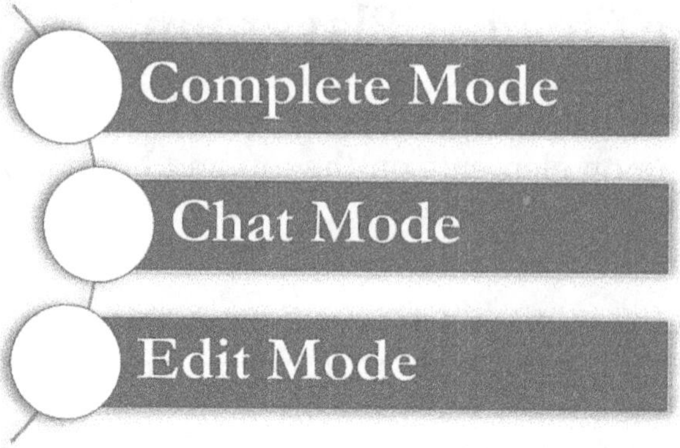

Figure 4-1 OpenAI ChatGPT Playground Interface Modes

B. Comparison of Different Modes

Following is a summary of the parameter settings available for different modes of the OpenAI Playground.

Playground Mode	Complete	Chat	Edit
Model	✓	✓	✓
Temperature	✓	✓	✓
Maximum length	✓	✓	
Stop sequences	✓		✓
Top P	✓	✓	✓
Frequency penalty	✓	✓	
Presence penalty	✓	✓	
Best of	✓		
Inject restart text	✓		
Show probabilities	✓		

These settings allow you to customize and control your interactions with ChatGPT in a myriad of powerful ways.

It is worth spending some time exploring these features to make the most of your experience with the model. You can then create and save presets for numerous custom interaction modes with ChatGPT.

C. Details of Playground Modes

1. Complete Mode

Imagine this as the mode similar to the Direct Interface but with the advantage of granular control over ChatGPT's responses using the panel on the right. As the name suggests, this Mode of the Playground provides the most control over ChatGPT responses.

Below is a description of the features of the Complete Mode.

1. **Input/Output area:** This is where you type in your prompts or queries for the model to respond to.

   The model's responses will appear in this area just below your message. You can have a continuous conversation with the model by adding more inputs, and it will maintain the context.

2. **Temperature slider**: This setting impacts the randomness of the model's responses. A higher temperature makes the output more diverse and potentially creative, while a lower temperature makes the output more focused and deterministic.

In simpler terms the "Temperature" setting is like the spice level for ChatGPT's responses. If you turn it up (closer to 2), ChatGPT's replies get spicier, or more diverse and potentially surprising. If you turn it down (closer to 0), ChatGPT's responses are plainer, sticking to safer, more predictable replies. So, it helps you control how much risk ChatGPT takes in its responses.

Needleless to say, if you would like a more fact-oriented response, it may be best to keep the temperature setting low.

Try setting the Temperature to a maximum allowed of 2. The response can become a scrambled, nonsensical paragraph with misspelled words. This outcome, while unusual, hints at the statistical nature underlying the advanced yet not quite human-like intelligence of current AI technology, reminding us that despite its revolutionary nature, there are still limitations to be explored.

3. **Maximum length slider**: This setting controls the maximum length of the response in terms of tokens[6]. You can adjust it based on how concise or detailed you want the model's answers to be. For instance, if you want a short response, you can set 'Maximum length' to a lower value like 50. This varies by the model selected. This can be a good way to manage your usage or to keep the responses succinct.

[6] A token is approximately 4 characters of normal English text.

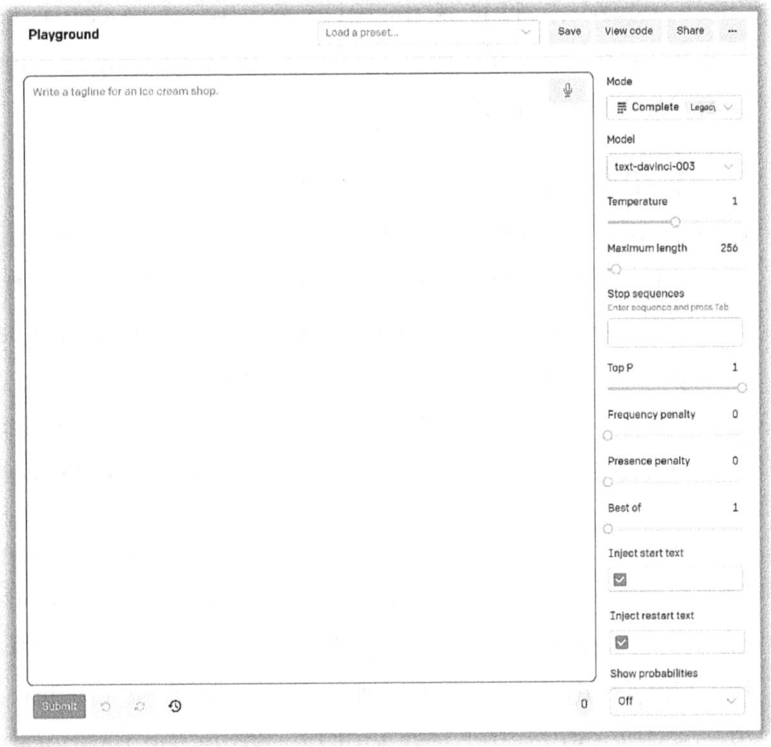

Figure 4-2 OpenAI ChatGPT Playground, Complete Mode

4. **Stop sequences text box**: As the name suggest, the "Stop sequences" text box is a feature that allows you to tell the model when to stop generating more text. You provide it with a specific sequence of characters or words, and when the model encounters this sequence in its output, it stops generating any further.

For example, let's say you are using the model to draft emails, and you always end your emails with "Best regards,". If you put "Best regards," in the "Stop sequences" box, the model will stop generating text as soon as it writes

"Best regards,". This is useful if you want to control the length of the text or if there is a particular ending sequence that you want the model to stop at.

5. **Top P slider**: The "Top P" setting is like a creativity dial for ChatGPT. If you turn it up (closer to 1), the responses become more varied and unpredictable. If you turn it down (closer to 0), the responses become more focused and predictable, sticking closer to what it considers the most likely next words. It helps control the balance between creativity and coherence in ChatGPT's replies.

   The "Top P" setting complements the "Temperature" setting, which also controls the randomness of the model's responses. However, the Top P parameter is different from the temperature setting because it sets how random or *diverse* the generated text will be, while the temperature setting affects how *confident* the generated text will be.

   Playing with these two parameters allows you to fine-tune the output of the GPT model according to your specific needs or preferences.

6. **Frequency penalty slider**: The "Frequency penalty" slider is a control that helps you influence how often ChatGPT uses common phrases. If you set it high (closer to 2), ChatGPT tries to avoid repeating common phrases, making its responses more varied and creative. If you set it low (closer to 0), it uses common phrases more frequently. So, it is like a dial for adjusting ChatGPT's originality in its responses.

Let's say you are asking ChatGPT to generate a sentence that describes a sunset.

With a low Frequency penalty (closer to 0), ChatGPT might generate a more typical sentence like:

```
The sunset was beautiful, painting the sky with shades of orange and pink.
```

With a high Frequency penalty (let's say 1.5), ChatGPT is encouraged to be more creative and avoid common phrases, leading to something like:

```
The sundown spectacle dazzled, splashing the firmament with a palette of tangerine and rose hues.
```

Think of it as – a higher frequency penalty tends to introduce a 'broader' detail with metaphorical or dynamic language.

You may find this to be a good setting to experiment with for creative writing assistance.

7. **Presence penalty slider**: The "Presence penalty" slider controls how much ChatGPT introduces new concepts in its responses. When set low (closer to 0), ChatGPT is encouraged to introduce new ideas, leading to more diverse and potentially longer responses. On the other hand, a high Presence Penalty (closer to 2) prompts ChatGPT to stick more closely to existing concepts, potentially yielding more concise and on-point responses.

Imagine asking ChatGPT to continue the sentence "I enjoy playing with my dog because...".

With a high Presence Penalty, ChatGPT may remain focused on the central theme (the enjoyment of playing with the dog), leading to something like:

```
I enjoy playing with my dog because it is a great way to bond with him, enjoy the outdoors, and it always brightens my day to see him having fun.
```

With a low Presence Penalty (closer to 0), ChatGPT could introduce additional concepts:

```
I enjoy playing with my dog because it's an excellent form of exercise, and it even becomes a meditation of sorts, putting me in touch with nature and the simple joys of life.
```

8. **Best of slider**: The "Best of" option in OpenAI's playground relates to how ChatGPT selects its final output from multiple possibilities.

When the model generates a response, it is not just creating one sentence and giving it to you. Behind the scenes, it is actually generating multiple possibilities based on this setting (a maximum of 20) and then choosing one to show based on its settings.

With "Best of", you are telling the model to generate a certain number of responses and then choose the "best" one according to its internal scoring mechanism. For example, if you set "Best of" to 5, the model generates 5 potential responses and then picks the one it determines is the best to display.

This can help improve the quality of the output by giving the model more chances to generate a good response. However, keep in mind that "best" is based on the model's trained understanding, which might not always align perfectly with human judgment.

It is also worth noting that increasing the "Best of" value can make the model slower, as it needs to generate more responses before it can return the final output.

CAUTION: Using the "Best of" option can impact usage and potentially incur more costs, depending on your usage plan with OpenAI.

This is because ChatGPT generates multiple potential responses and each one is considered an individual usage of the model. So, if you set "Best of" to 5, it is equivalent to using the model 5 times, and you will be charged accordingly.

The exact details of how this affects billing may vary, so I would recommend checking OpenAI's latest documentation.

9. **Inject start text**: The "Inject start text" setting allows you to provide a specific text input at the beginning of each generated message from ChatGPT to format the model for a response.

Consider it as giving ChatGPT a certain quick “direction” or "mindset" or "personality" that persists throughout the conversation. The text is appended to the user’s prompt automatically.

Consider the following interaction with the setting of Inject start text set to “ Based in,”:

> **User**: What is the tallest man-made structure in the world? **Based in,**
>
> **ChatGPT**: Based in Dubai, United Arab Emirates, the tallest man-made structure in the world is the Burj Khalifa tower. It stands at 828 meters (2,717 feet) tall and was completed in 2010.

Now consider the following interaction with the setting of Inject start text set to “ In the language of Shakespeare,”:

> **User**: What is the tallest man-made structure in the world? **In the language of Shakespeare,**
>
> **ChatGPT:** The grandest man-made structure e'er forged is the lofty Burj Khalifa, set within the city of Dubai. It doth ascend a full two thousand and seven hundred and seventy-

```
three feet, twas a veritable marvel of modern engineering.


   User: What is special about it?  In the language of Shakespeare,

   ChatGPT: This remarkable edifice is an awe-inspiring feat of engineering prowess, which stands as a testament to mankind's capacity to stretch his reach to the limits of nature's bounty. Its height of two-thousand-seven-hundred and seventy-two metres is a sight that astonishes those fortunate enough to behold it.
```

The Inject start text is applied to every message from ChatGPT, so it can have an impact on the conversation's direction and style. Sometimes the provided start text may have no impact as well if it is too simple, redundant or illogical.

10. **Inject restart text**: The "Inject restart text" feature allows you to specify a text that resets the context for ChatGPT and starts a new conversation. This could be useful when you want to change the direction of a conversation or the role ChatGPT is playing.

For example, suppose you want to ask ChatGPT about Shakespeare and would like to contrast the response with similar fact about Mark Twain. The interaction may be something like:

> **Inject Restart text value**: Whereas Mark Twain
>
> **User**: Tell me 1 interesting fact about Shakespeare.
>
> **ChatGPT:** Shakespeare has been translated into more than 80 languages and is performed more often than any other playwright Whereas Mark Twain's novels are the most-translated American works.

The "Inject restart text" setting is useful in scenarios where you want to change the context or role of ChatGPT in the middle of a conversation. Here are a few examples where it could come in handy:

- Role-playing Games, Simulations, Debates etc.: You might be using ChatGPT to simulate different characters or points of view. The "Inject restart text" can help you switch roles or contexts without starting a new conversation.

- Creative Writing or Storytelling: If you are using ChatGPT to help generate ideas for a story or a screenplay, you might want it to switch between different characters or plotlines.

- Versatile Assistance: If you are using ChatGPT as a general-purpose assistant, there might be times where you want it to switch from a casual to a more formal one.

11. **Show probabilities dropdown**: The "Show probabilities" feature in the OpenAI Playground is a technical feature that might not be necessary for everyday usage. Feel free to skip this section. This may however help a savvy user debug a given response or see alternative options in terms of probabilities.

    The response is *highlighted in different color shades* for a quick view. Upon clicking a word, a drop down shows its probability versus probabilities of other words that ChatGPT considered. It also shows probabilities on a logarithmic[7] scale.

    From the drop down you can choose three ways to view the probabilities.

    - Most Likely: When you select this and generate a response, ChatGPT will display the tokens (words or parts of words) that were most probable given its understanding of the context. This can be useful to see what it considers the most "natural".

    - Least Likely: In contrast, the "Least Likely" option will show the tokens that had the lowest probability

[7] ChatGPT shows "logprob" which stands for log probability. This term is used in the context of natural language processing and machine learning, particularly in generative models like ChatGPT. It represents the natural logarithm of the probability the model assigned to each token (word or piece of a word) in the response. For example, if a particular token had a logprob of -1, this means ChatGPT assigned a probability of e^{-1} (approximately 0.367) to that token at that step in generating the response. The higher the logprob, the more "likely" the token was picked, given the context ChatGPT was working from.

according to ChatGPT. This might reveal some very interesting or unusual tokens, as these are the tokens that ChatGPT assessed as least likely from the provided context.

- Full Spectrum: This option displays a broad range of tokens, encompassing both the most likely and least likely outputs. By viewing the full spectrum, you can see a wide variety of possible tokens and how ChatGPT ranks their likelihoods.

  Let's Consider two examples with the "Full spectrum" setting.

Example 1: Suppose you ask a factual question

```
User: What is the capital of Japan?

ChatGPT: The capital of Japan is Tokyo.
```

The response is so unambiguous, the response on the screen will reveal only a few shades of color.

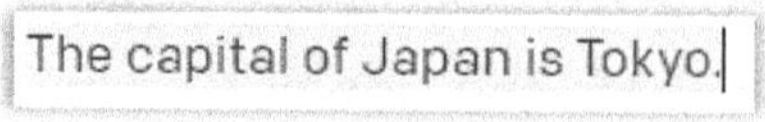

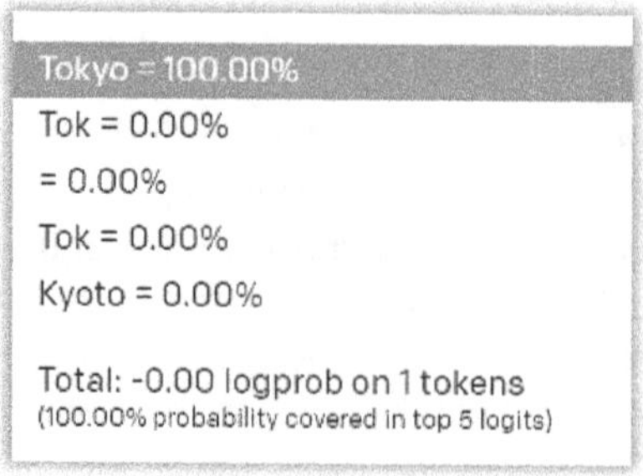

Clicking on the word "Tokyo" displays 100% probability, showing ChatGPT's confidence that its response is correct based on its training data

Example 2: Suppose you ask a subjective question:

```
User: What is the best flavor of ice cream?

ChatGPT: This is a matter of personal preference, so there is no single "best" flavor of ice cream. Some popular flavors include vanilla, chocolate, strawberry, mint chocolate chip, rocky road, butter pecan, and cookie dough.
```

The response has uncertainty, so the response on the screen will reveal several shades.

This is a matter of personal preference, so there is no single "best" flavor of ice cream. Some popular flavors include vanilla, chocolate, strawberry, mint chocolate chip, rocky road, butter pecan, and cookie dough.

Clicking on the word chocolate reveals a higher probability vs for Strawberry.

chocolate = 92.39%
strawberry = 7.30%
mint = 0.11%
cookie = 0.06%
cookies = 0.05%

Total: -0.08 logprob on 1 tokens
(99.91% probability covered in top 5 logits)

It shows that ChatGPT is more confident in chocolate vs strawberry in its response, reflecting the subjectivity of the question.

It is interesting to note here that ChatGPT does not know what chocolate or strawberry flavors mean. It just weighs the probabilities across different possible responses based on its training. This point becomes clearer if you click on "pecan" which shows 100% probability as well since it is the most likely word to follow "butter" in the context of "butter pecan" ice cream.

If you are very curious, playing with this setting and different prompts can reveal a lot about how language models like ChatGPT work.

12. **Load a preset dropdown**: The "Load a preset" function in the OpenAI Playground allows you to quickly load a predefined set of parameters for ChatGPT model. These presets are designed to help you achieve certain types of responses or behaviors from ChatGPT without having to manually adjust each individual parameter every time.

    For example, you might save a preset for "Creative Writing" with a high temperature and a low Presence penalty as well as some other parameters to encourage ChatGPT to assume a certain writing format or style.

    On the other hand, there might be a "Technical Explanation" preset that adjusts parameters to make ChatGPT give detailed, focused, and technical responses suitable for explaining complex concepts or topics e.g., a lower Temperature setting and a higher Presence penalty etc.

By using the "Load a Preset" function, you can easily switch between different modes of interaction and a combination of settings for ChatGPT, depending on what you need from it at the moment. This can be a very useful feature if you want to save various personas for AI assistants that suit various aspects of your style or areas of work.

It is worth noting that you are not restricted to the presets. You can still manually adjust the parameters after loading a preset if you wish to further fine-tune ChatGPT's behavior.

13. **Save button**: Saves (or updates) the current settings to the selected Preset. Alternatively, you can use a keyboard shortcut Ctrl+s (Windows) or control+s (Mac).

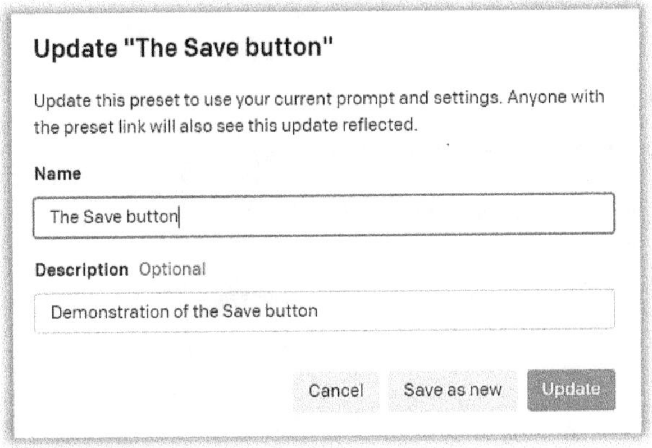

14. **View code button**: This button provides the complete code corresponding to your current interaction that runs behind the scenes to connect with the ChatGPT model, using an API call. This can be useful for developers wanting to understand how to make similar calls programmatically.

15. **Share button:** This is perhaps one of the most useful features of the Playground in terms of collaboration.

    When you click the "Share" button, it generates a unique URL that you can use to share the current state of your Playground session with others. This includes the input prompts you have used *and* the responses generated by ChatGPT. When anyone with this link opens the link, they will see the same Playground session as you do *but within their account.*

    This functionality can be helpful for demonstrating a specific use case, time saving, troubleshooting, or collaborating with a colleague or friend.

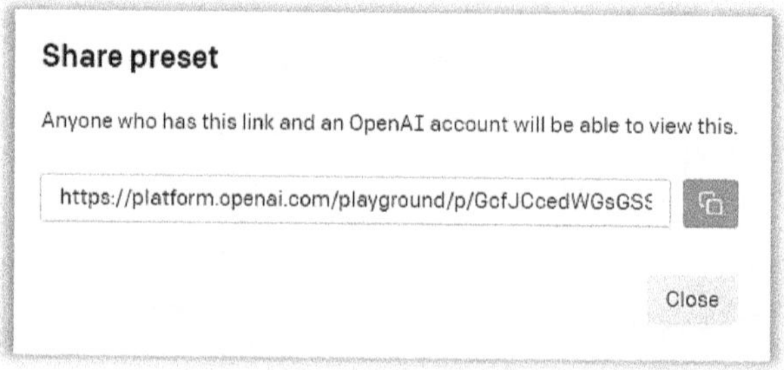

Your colleague or friend, can change their version of the preset, save it under a different name and share forward or share it back with you.

16. **Ellipses button**: Currently, this shows dropdown options to delete your current preset and update Content filter preferences setting.

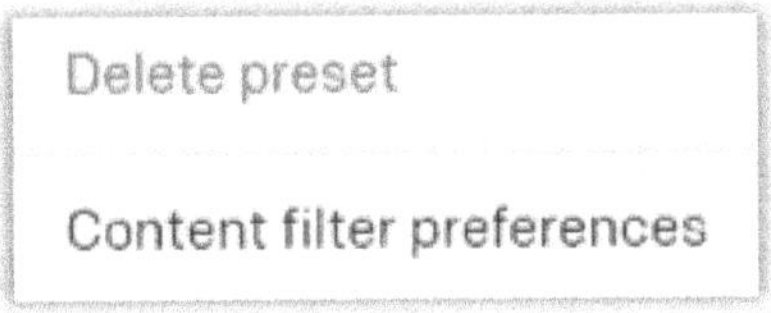

Clicking the Delete preset link presents you with the option to delete your current preset. This will delete the preset from your account and will not be accessible by anyone who you have shared it with unless they have saved it as their own preset.

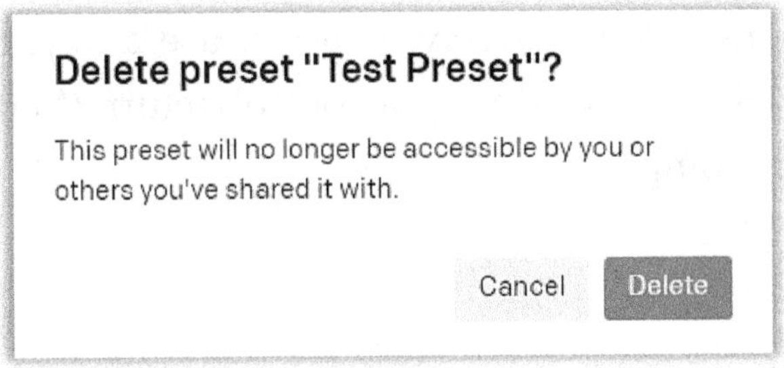

The Content filter preferences allow you to see warnings for content that is inappropriate per OpenAI policies.

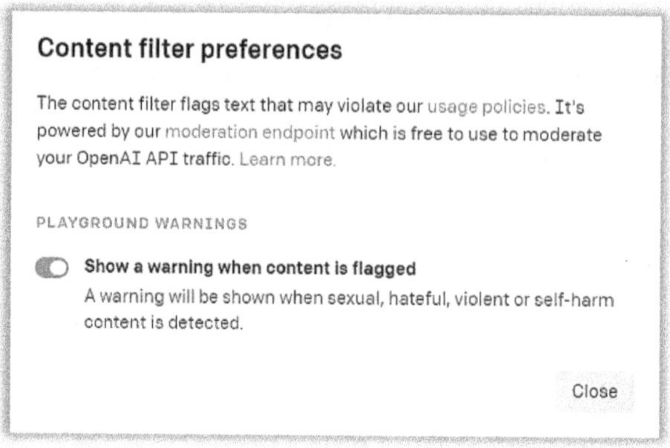

While the warnings can be turned off, your usage of ChatGPT remains subject to all OpenAI terms that you agree to when you sign up for your OpenAI account.

17. **Submit Button**: This submits your text to ChatGPT to elicit a response. Alternatively, you can use a keyboard shortcut Ctrl+Enter (Windows) or control+return (Mac) to submit your prompt.

18. **Undo Last Button**: Allows you to undo the last response from ChatGPT. Alternatively, you can use a keyboard shortcut Ctrl+u (Windows) or control+u (Mac). This is disabled until you start your chat. 

19. **Regenerate Button**: This regenerates your last interaction with ChatGPT. This is disabled until you start your chat.

Alternatively, you can use a keyboard shortcut Ctrl+Enter (Windows) or control+return (Mac).

20. **Chat history**: The OpenAI Playground maintains a chat history. You can scroll up to see previous interactions in your current session. If you have restarted the chat, then you can see your chat history by clicking on the clock icon at the bottom.

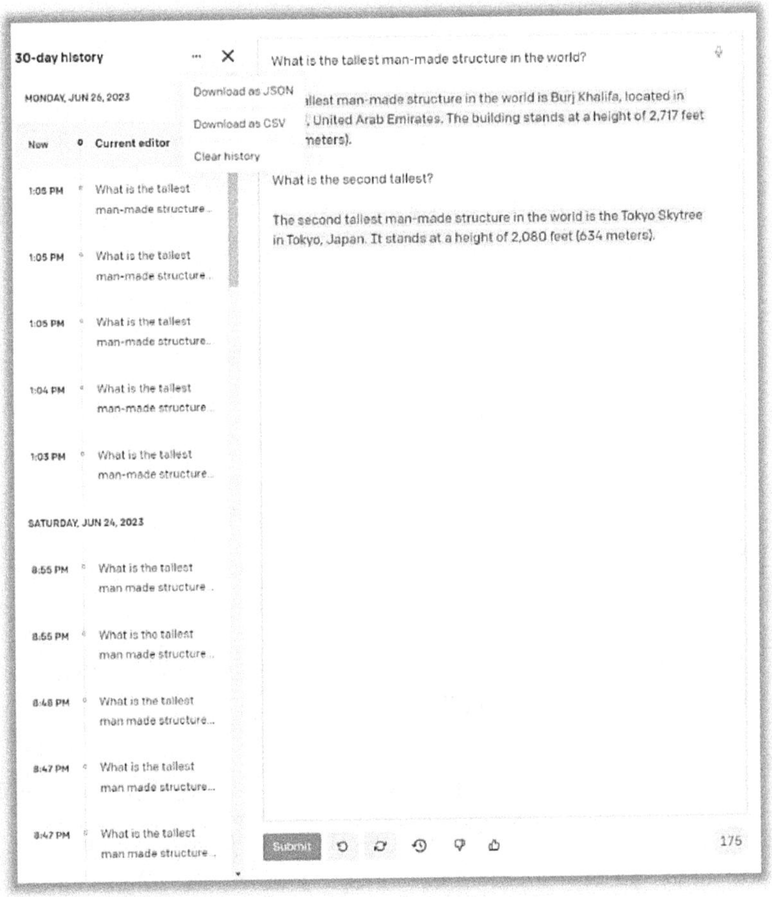

Figure 4-3 ChatGPT Playground with Chat History

21. **Feedback buttons**: These provide you the ability to provide quick feedback on the responses generated. This helps OpenAI improve a model's performance.

22. **Speech to text**: The mic icon in the text input area allows you to upload audio from your computer or record your prompt using speech.

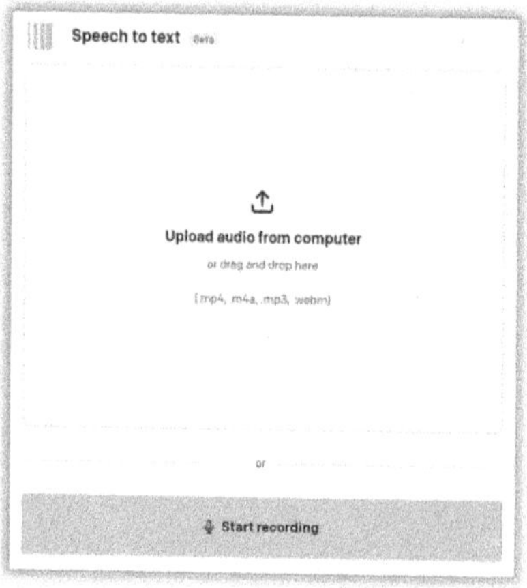

2. Chat Mode

This is one of the most useful features of the Playground, where you can engage ChatGPT in role-playing.

At the time the writing of this book, Chat mode is in beta (experimental) stage. However, it is quite feature rich.

It includes a "SYSTEM" text box where you can establish an overall context for ChatGPT to frame its responses. For instance, you might set the context as:

- You are a helpful assistant
- You are the best editor
- You are a math teacher for 4th grade
- You are a molecular biologist who can break down hard concepts to explain to 2-year-olds.

And so on. The possibilities are endless!

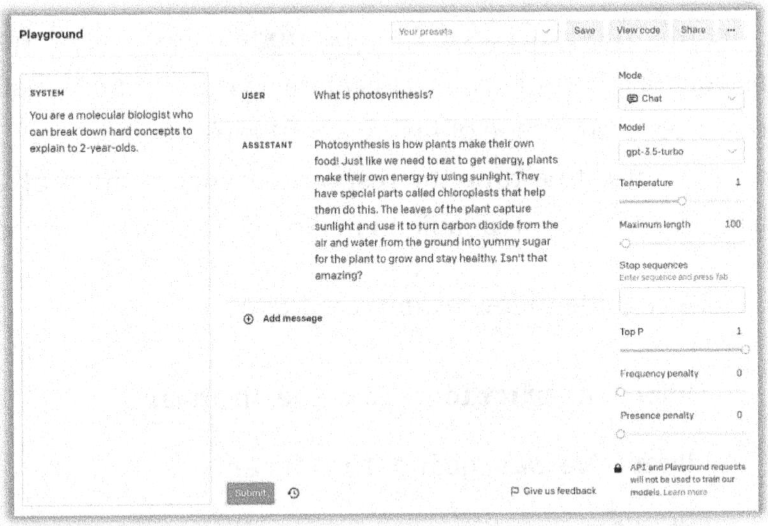

Figure 4-4 OpenAI ChatGPT Playground, Chat Mode

Similar context-setting can be done in the direct ChatGPT interface at the start of your chat. However, the Playground's role-defining feature simplifies this. In normal chats, ChatGPT has a token limit determining how much context it can remember when responding. If the conversation exceeds this limit, some initial context may be 'forgotten.' By setting a role in Playground, the context is firmly anchored, remaining intact even when the token limit is reached. In the direct ChatGPT interface, context management and occasional reminders are necessary.

Please note that several of the settings that are available in the Complete mode, are not available in the Chat mode as they are not applicable. Please see the comparison table in the previous section B.

3. Edit Mode

In this mode ChatGPT helps update text based on the instructions you provide. This allows you to direct ChatGPT to one particular type of task without repeating yourself. You can of course fine tune the response in many different ways using the settings available to make this feature quite useful.

Let's consider a few examples:

```
User Instruction: Fix the grammar.

User: We was going to soccer.

ChatGPT: We are going to soccer
```

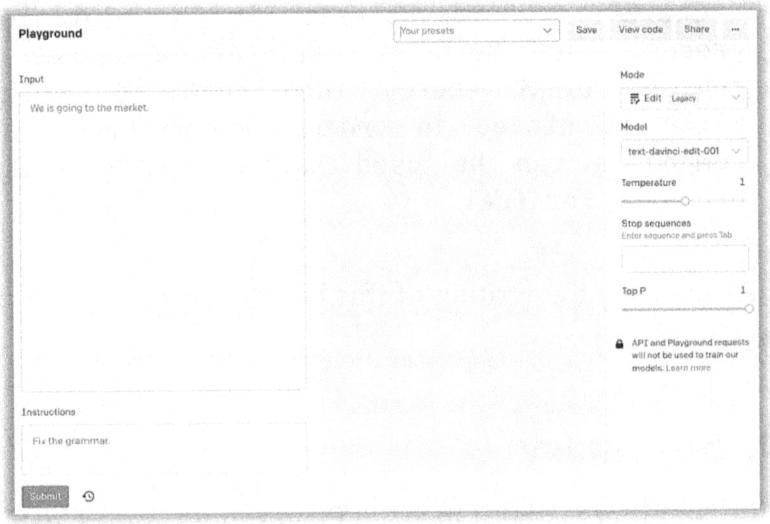

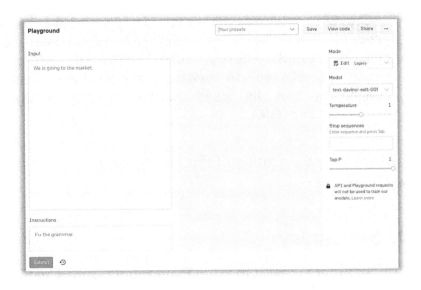

Figure 4-5 OpenAI ChatGPT Playground, Edit Mode

Now let's take a slightly more complex example:

```
User Instruction: Summarize for a second grader.

User: Photosynthesis is a biological process used by many cellular organisms to convert light energy into chemical energy, which is stored in organic compounds that can later be metabolized through cellular respiration to fuel the organism's activities. The term usually refers to oxygenic photosynthesis, where oxygen is produced as a byproduct, and some of the chemical energy produced is stored in carbohydrate molecules such as sugars, starch and cellulose, which are synthesized from endergonic reaction of carbon dioxide with water.
```

```
ChatGPT: Photosynthesis is a biological process used by many cellular organisms to convert light energy into chemical energy, which is stored in organic compounds. These compounds can be used later by any living organism for fuel.
```

At the time the writing of this book, Edit mode is in beta (experimental) stage.

D. Summary

In summary, the OpenAI Playground and ChatGPT interface each have their unique features and use cases. The Playground is ideal for experimentation, testing various models, and adjusting settings, while the ChatGPT interface provides a more focused and simple conversation-based experience. By understanding the differences between these platforms, you will be better equipped to choose the right tool for your specific needs.

Next, we will explore crafting effective prompts to amplify your effectiveness and expertise with ChatGPT.

5. Crafting Effective Prompts

In the field of AI, prompts play a vital role, particularly in language models such as ChatGPT. Prompts are snippets of text used to spur the model into generating a response that aligns with its training data and the specifics outlined by the prompt. In essence, the text generation process in ChatGPT is initiated by prompts.

The nature of prompts can vary widely, depending on the user's objective. They could range from simple questions or assertions to short stories, tasks, or broad themes. The complexity of prompts can range from a single word to detailed essays. However, an effective prompt should be specific, clear, and provide sufficient background information for ChatGPT to grasp the context and generate a relevant response.

For example, a question like "Can you give me a recipe for chocolate chip cookies?" is likely to produce a more focused response than "Can you provide me a baking recipe?”. Similarly, a prompt such as "Narrate a short story about a robot that wakes up" furnishes ChatGPT with enough context to create a short story based on the given premise.

A. Prompt Design and Prompt Engineering

The way prompts are articulated can notably impact the efficacy and relevance of ChatGPT responses. This involves the strategic composition of prompts to direct ChatGPT towards generating the desired type of response. It can involve detailing the format you want the answer in, giving context, or instructing ChatGPT to deliberate step-by-step or weigh pros and cons before settling on a conclusion.

The art of thoughtfully curating prompts to coax out the most satisfactory responses from ChatGPT is often described as "**prompt engineering**" or "**prompt design**".

"Prompt engineering" and "Prompt design" are terms that are often used interchangeably in the context of language models like ChatGPT. Both refer to the process of carefully crafting prompts to elicit desirable and effective responses from the model.

However, there can be slight nuances between the two:

"Prompt Design" typically refers to the overall process of constructing a prompt: determining what information to include, how to phrase the prompt, what format to use, etc., with the goal of guiding ChatGPT to produce a specific type

2. **Employ Specificity in Your Writing**: More precise prompts tend to produce more useful responses. Rather than posing a general question, provide specific instructions or ask for a particular kind of information. For example,

    - Specific Prompt: "What is the Pythagorean theorem, and can you provide an example of how to use it?".

      This prompt is clear, specific, and directly asks for information along with an example.

    - Unclear Prompt: "Tell me about the latest developments in technology.".

      While this prompt may seem clear, it's actually quite vague due to its broad scope as it could refer to a wide variety of fields, like AI, robotics, biotechnology etc.

3. **Utilize Clear Language**: Clarity is paramount when constructing a prompt. Refrain from using jargon or intricate terms that might confuse ChatGPT. The quality of the model's response hinges on the quality of the input data. Hence, if your prompt is ambiguous, the response will likely be too. For example,

    - Unclear Prompt: "Can you elucidate the esoteric elements of the Cartesian dualism hypothesis?".

      This prompt uses overly complex language and jargon, which might confuse ChatGPT.

    - Clear Prompt: "Can you explain the concept of dualism as proposed by René Descartes?".

of response. It is about structuring your request in a way that ChatGPT understands and responds effectively.

"Prompt Engineering" is a term that can encompass prompt design, but may also imply an iterative process of experimenting with different prompts, measuring their effectiveness, and refining them based on feedback or data. This could include testing multiple versions of prompts, analyzing the performance of different prompts, and systematically improving them over time.

Again, these are subtle differences and the terms are often used to mean the same thing. In both cases, the ultimate goal is to optimize the interactions with ChatGPT model to achieve the best possible results.

B. Cordiality in Prompts

Although ChatGPT lacks emotions and does not demand courtesy as a human does, employing polite language in your prompts can still be advantageous. It fosters a pleasant ambiance for interaction, may influence the tone of the responses, and often enhances the specificity of your prompts.

C. Prompt Categories

Various types of prompts find their use in AI models. Here are five key categories:

Figure 5-1 Prompt Categories

1. **Question Prompts**: These are designed to obtain certain specific information or responses. Examples include "What is the capital of Iceland?" or "Can you explain solar energy?".
2. **Completion Prompts**: These provide ChatGPT with an initial fragment of text and instruct it to complete the text. For instance, "It was a dark, stormy night, and he felt…" or "Some of the benefits of running are…".
3. **Story Prompts**: These prompts guide ChatGPT to weave a story or narrative around a particular topic or theme. For example, "Compose a short story about a tree that talks " or "Develop a mystery tale set in a New York subway.".
4. **Dialogue Prompts**: These prompts guide ChatGPT to simulate conversations between characters in a designated scenario or setting. Examples include, "Simulate a conversation between a customer and a support specialist" or "Craft a dialogue between two friends discussing benefits of exercising.".

5. **Creative Prompts**: These are open-ended prompts that stimulate ChatGPT to create unique outputs like a poem, song, or script. For instance, "Pen a poem about joy" or "Compose a script for a comedy film about a boy who likes to swim.".

D. Building Effective Prompts

The task of creating effective prompts for AI models can be daunting. However, by adhering to certain guidelines, you can design prompts that assist the AI model in generating high-quality, relevant responses. Here is an in-depth guide on constructing potent prompts for AI models:

1. **Define the Task and Objective of Your Prompt**: Before writing your prompt, decide what task you want ChatGPT to perform and what the intended outcome is. Are you searching for information, a narrative, or a unique creative output? With a solid understanding of the task and the goal of your prompt, writing a specific and context-relevant prompt becomes easier.

   For example, "Can you create a short poem about a sunset on the beach? The objective is to evoke a sense of peace and tranquility.".

   In this prompt, the task (creating a short poem about sunset on the beach) as well as the objective (to evoke sense of peace and tranquility - the intended mood tone) are well defined.

This revised prompt conveys the same request in much simpler and clearer language.

4. **Furnish Context**: Context is key when crafting a prompt. For a relevant response, ChatGPT needs to grasp what the prompt is about. Supply it with enough background information to help it comprehend the situation or topic you are presenting.

   For example, "In the context of the novel 'To Kill a Mockingbird', can you explain the significance of the mockingbird symbol?".

   In this prompt, the context (the novel 'To Kill a Mockingbird') is very clear.

5. **Consider Prompt Length**: The length of the prompt can influence the response quality. While a longer prompt can provide more context and details, your intention or real question may become unclear. On the other hand, a shorter prompt might be easier for ChatGPT but might not provide enough information for a substantial response. For example,

   - Long Prompt: "I have been reading about ancient civilizations, particularly those around the Mediterranean Sea. I've learned about the Greeks, Romans, and Carthaginians. One thing that has caught my interest is the extensive trade routes they established. In the context of these civilizations, especially during the height of their powers, can you explain the major commodities they traded and the impact of these trade routes on their economic prosperity?".

While this prompt provides lots of contexts, it may be unclear for ChatGPT to discern the main question due to the length and complexity of the sentence.

- Short Prompt: "Can you tell me about Ancient trade routes in the Mediterranean Sea?".

  This shorter prompt is easier for ChatGPT to process, but it lacks sufficient detail and context.

- Balanced Prompt: "Can you explain the major commodities traded along ancient Mediterranean trade routes and their economic impact?".

  This revised prompt is more balanced in length. It is not overly lengthy but still provides enough detail and context for ChatGPT for a focused response.

6. **Dictate the Format**: If you desire the answer in a specific format, include that in your prompt.

   For example, "Can you give me a three-bullet-point summary of the main functions of the United Nations?".

   This prompt not only asks for information about the United Nations, but it also specifies the format for the response clearly.

7. **Experiment and Iterate**: Don't hesitate to experiment with different prompt styles. If you are not receiving the response you desire, try rewording your prompt or

of response. It is about structuring your request in a way that ChatGPT understands and responds effectively.

"Prompt Engineering" is a term that can encompass prompt design, but may also imply an iterative process of experimenting with different prompts, measuring their effectiveness, and refining them based on feedback or data. This could include testing multiple versions of prompts, analyzing the performance of different prompts, and systematically improving them over time.

Again, these are subtle differences and the terms are often used to mean the same thing. In both cases, the ultimate goal is to optimize the interactions with ChatGPT model to achieve the best possible results.

B. Cordiality in Prompts

Although ChatGPT lacks emotions and does not demand courtesy as a human does, employing polite language in your prompts can still be advantageous. It fosters a pleasant ambiance for interaction, may influence the tone of the responses, and often enhances the specificity of your prompts.

C. Prompt Categories

Various types of prompts find their use in AI models. Here are five key categories:

Figure 5-1 Prompt Categories

1. **Question Prompts**: These are designed to obtain certain specific information or responses. Examples include "What is the capital of Iceland?" or "Can you explain solar energy?".
2. **Completion Prompts**: These provide ChatGPT with an initial fragment of text and instruct it to complete the text. For instance, "It was a dark, stormy night, and he felt…" or "Some of the benefits of running are…".
3. **Story Prompts**: These prompts guide ChatGPT to weave a story or narrative around a particular topic or theme. For example, "Compose a short story about a tree that talks " or "Develop a mystery tale set in a New York subway.".
4. **Dialogue Prompts**: These prompts guide ChatGPT to simulate conversations between characters in a designated scenario or setting. Examples include, "Simulate a conversation between a customer and a support specialist" or "Craft a dialogue between two friends discussing benefits of exercising.".

5. **Creative Prompts**: These are open-ended prompts that stimulate ChatGPT to create unique outputs like a poem, song, or script. For instance, "Pen a poem about joy" or "Compose a script for a comedy film about a boy who likes to swim.".

D. Building Effective Prompts

The task of creating effective prompts for AI models can be daunting. However, by adhering to certain guidelines, you can design prompts that assist the AI model in generating high-quality, relevant responses. Here is an in-depth guide on constructing potent prompts for AI models:

1. **Define the Task and Objective of Your Prompt**: Before writing your prompt, decide what task you want ChatGPT to perform and what the intended outcome is. Are you searching for information, a narrative, or a unique creative output? With a solid understanding of the task and the goal of your prompt, writing a specific and context-relevant prompt becomes easier.

   For example, "Can you create a short poem about a sunset on the beach? The objective is to evoke a sense of peace and tranquility.".

   In this prompt, the task (creating a short poem about a sunset on the beach) as well as the objective (to evoke a sense of peace and tranquility - the intended mood or tone) are well defined.

2. **Employ Specificity in Your Writing**: More precise prompts tend to produce more useful responses. Rather than posing a general question, provide specific instructions or ask for a particular kind of information. For example,

   - Specific Prompt: "What is the Pythagorean theorem, and can you provide an example of how to use it?".

     This prompt is clear, specific, and directly asks for information along with an example.

   - Unclear Prompt: "Tell me about the latest developments in technology.".

     While this prompt may seem clear, it's actually quite vague due to its broad scope as it could refer to a wide variety of fields, like AI, robotics, biotechnology etc.

3. **Utilize Clear Language**: Clarity is paramount when constructing a prompt. Refrain from using jargon or intricate terms that might confuse ChatGPT. The quality of the model's response hinges on the quality of the input data. Hence, if your prompt is ambiguous, the response will likely be too. For example,

   - Unclear Prompt: "Can you elucidate the esoteric elements of the Cartesian dualism hypothesis?".

     This prompt uses overly complex language and jargon, which might confuse ChatGPT.

   - Clear Prompt: "Can you explain the concept of dualism as proposed by René Descartes?".

This revised prompt conveys the same request in much simpler and clearer language.

4. **Furnish Context**: Context is key when crafting a prompt. For a relevant response, ChatGPT needs to grasp what the prompt is about. Supply it with enough background information to help it comprehend the situation or topic you are presenting.

   For example, "In the context of the novel 'To Kill a Mockingbird', can you explain the significance of the mockingbird symbol?".

   In this prompt, the context (the novel 'To Kill a Mockingbird') is very clear.

5. **Consider Prompt Length**: The length of the prompt can influence the response quality. While a longer prompt can provide more context and details, your intention or real question may become unclear. On the other hand, a shorter prompt might be easier for ChatGPT but might not provide enough information for a substantial response. For example,

   - Long Prompt: "I have been reading about ancient civilizations, particularly those around the Mediterranean Sea. I've learned about the Greeks, Romans, and Carthaginians. One thing that has caught my interest is the extensive trade routes they established. In the context of these civilizations, especially during the height of their powers, can you explain the major commodities they traded and the impact of these trade routes on their economic prosperity?".

While this prompt provides lots of contexts, it may be unclear for ChatGPT to discern the main question due to the length and complexity of the sentence.

- Short Prompt: "Can you tell me about Ancient trade routes in the Mediterranean Sea?".

  This shorter prompt is easier for ChatGPT to process, but it lacks sufficient detail and context.

- Balanced Prompt: "Can you explain the major commodities traded along ancient Mediterranean trade routes and their economic impact?".

  This revised prompt is more balanced in length. It is not overly lengthy but still provides enough detail and context for ChatGPT for a focused response.

6. **Dictate the Format**: If you desire the answer in a specific format, include that in your prompt.

   For example, "Can you give me a three-bullet-point summary of the main functions of the United Nations?".

   This prompt not only asks for information about the United Nations, but it also specifies the format for the response clearly.

7. **Experiment and Iterate**: Don't hesitate to experiment with different prompt styles. If you are not receiving the response you desire, try rewording your prompt or

adding more detail. Repeat this process until you achieve the desired output.

Creating effective prompts is a skill honed with practice. The more you interact with ChatGPT, the more adept you become at formulating prompts that extract the responses you desire.

E. Mastery in Prompt Construction: Enhanced Tactics

Becoming proficient in formulating effective prompts for AI systems is a union of art and science. This skill can unlock a wide array of creative, informative, and engaging interactions. Here are some enhanced strategies and techniques to guide you in this endeavor.

1. **Ask ChatGPT to Rephrase Text**: You can use existing text from other sources as prompts for the AI, like ChatGPT, to process. It can simplify complex scientific explanations, translate text into different languages, or even spruce up a dull paragraph.
2. **Engage in Role Play**: Role-playing with ChatGPT can yield enjoyable and insightful interactions. ChatGPT model can impersonate a myriad of characters, from an emoji-filled teen to a historical figure like Abraham Lincoln. This versatile role-play feature serves both entertainment and educational purposes.
3. **ChatGPT's Balanced Viewpoints**: ChatGPT's capability to argue both sides of an argument can help you explore

any topic deeper and appreciate its various facets. Be it politics, philosophy, arts, or sports, ChatGPT excels at presenting balanced perspectives.

4. **Provide Example Data**: Supplying ChatGPT with examples or a dataset before posing your question can markedly enhance the output. For example, you could feed a list of book summaries with their genres, and then ask ChatGPT to categorize a new summary.

5. **Limit ChatGPT's Responses**: Restricting responses can sometimes generate more fascinating outputs. You might confine ChatGPT to respond within a limited number of words or paragraphs, or to use words no longer than seven characters. This prompts ChatGPT to craft concise yet complete responses.

6. **Use ChatGPT to Assist with Other AI Models**: ChatGPT can also help generate innovative and practical prompts for other AI tools like Dall-E and Midjourney. By clarifying what you are seeking or even feeding it the format and examples of prompts for those tools, ChatGPT can provide suggestions that can be further used with these other AI tools.

7. **Ask ChatGPT to use Emoji's**: Though primarily text-oriented, ChatGPT can generate emoji's when prompted. This is particularly useful and fun if you are using ChatGPT to write social media content.

8. **Request Tabulated Responses**: ChatGPT's ability to generate responses in table format is a handy feature. It can organize information in a more digestible and

structured manner, such as tabulating meal ideas and their ingredients or comparing the pronunciation of weekdays in different languages.

9. **Specify Your Audience**: Adapting ChatGPT's responses to fit a specific audience is another effective tactic. Whether you are conversing with ten-year-olds or business entrepreneurs, informing ChatGPT about the audience helps it tailor its responses accordingly.
10. **Ask ChatGPT to Write in a Different Style**: Requesting ChatGPT to mimic a certain writing style can lend a unique flair to its output. You might ask it to emulate the distinctive style of your favorite author, like Erma Bombeck's funny prose or Shakespeare's lyrical verses.
11. **Encourage ChatGPT to Provide Comprehensive Answers**: Asking ChatGPT for a comprehensive answer, providing it with various 'ingredients' to work with, can lead to more elaborate and creative responses. This could involve suggesting a recipe based on available ingredients or creating a murder mystery scenario with a given set of characters.
12. **Ask ChatGPT to Verify its Understanding of Instructions or Results**: For complex tasks, it can be beneficial to phrase your prompt in a way that asks ChatGPT to confirm its interpretation of the task before proceeding with a detailed response. This approach can help to steer its response in the right direction from the outset, reducing the need for multiple iterations.

Interestingly, asking ChatGPT to explain the reasoning behind its response can sometimes yield additional or clarified information. While this is not indicative of consciousness or true understanding on its part, it is a way of formulating prompts that might lead it to generate more accurate or comprehensive output based on the patterns it learned during training

Mastering prompt formulation involves understanding ChatGPT's capabilities, crafting thoughtful prompts, considering the audience, and an eagerness to learn and improve through feedback and iteration.

F. Important Consideration

When utilizing ChatGPT, while crafting effective prompts plays a significant role, the process can be greatly simplified and enhanced by applying the techniques discussed in this chapter within the OpenAI playground. The playground offers numerous parameters to fine-tune ChatGPT's responses. Leveraging these tools will enable you to generate more customized and precise responses, thereby reducing the effort required in formulating prompts, as the need to manage all aspects within the text of your prompts will be lessened.

G. Summary

In summary, crafting effective text prompts requires a thorough understanding of an AI model's capabilities and limitations, particularly for models like ChatGPT. It is essential to consider the context and audience, use precise and unambiguous language, and commit to a process of continual testing and refinement. By adhering to these principles, you can create prompts that significantly improve the accuracy and quality of AI text generation.

Specifically, for ChatGPT the combination of well-designed prompts and the effective utilization of tools like the OpenAI Playground can unlock a wide range of ChatGPT's potential, generating more insightful and reliable responses.

6. Ethics and Responsible Use of ChatGPT and AI

As we reach deeper into the world of artificial intelligence and explore the capabilities of ChatGPT, it is important to consider the ethical implications and responsibilities that come with using such a powerful tool. This chapter aims to shed some light on the ethical considerations when using AI, potential misuse, and OpenAI's use-case policy.

A. Understanding AI Ethics

AI ethics is an emerging branch of ethics that examines the impact of AI and its implications on society. It involves considering questions about fairness, transparency, privacy, and accountability. When using ChatGPT, it is important to remember that while it is a tool designed to assist and enhance human capabilities, it should be used responsibly and ethically due to its expansive capabilities.

B. Potential Misuse of AI

AI, including ChatGPT, may be misused in several ways. For instance, AI, in general, may be used to generate misleading or false information, create deepfake media – such as text, images, video, audio – or automate spam messages. It is also possible for AI to inadvertently perpetuate biases present in the data it was trained on, leading to unfair or discriminatory outcomes.

As users of AI, we must be vigilant about these potential misuses and strive to use AI tools like ChatGPT responsibly. This means using ChatGPT to generate content that is truthful, respectful, and fair, and not using it to deceive, harm, or discriminate against others.

C. OpenAI's Use-Case Policy

OpenAI has established a use-case policy to guide the responsible use of its AI models, including ChatGPT. This policy prohibits uses of the AI that are harmful or violate laws or regulations. It also prohibits uses that involve deception, harassment, or other forms of harm or discrimination.

As users of ChatGPT, it is important to familiarize ourselves with OpenAI's use-case policy and ensure that our use of ChatGPT aligns with these guidelines. This not only helps prevent misuse of ChatGPT, but also contributes to a more ethical and responsible AI user community.

D. The Role of Transparency in AI Ethics

Transparency in AI refers to the ability to understand how an AI system makes decisions and produces content. This is particularly relevant with models like ChatGPT, which can generate complex outputs. Understanding how these decisions are made can help ensure that AI is being used ethically and responsibly. It can also help identify and correct biases in AI outputs, and increase accountability.

Due to how current AI models are constructed and trained, it is difficult to establish the precise sources of information that went into their responses. Ongoing research in the field of AI aims to increase transparency in the responses generated by models like ChatGPT. Regardless, it is recommended to always verify that no legal and ethical guidelines or regulations have been inadvertently breached when using content generated by AI/ChatGPT.

E. The Importance of Data Privacy

Data privacy is a key ethical consideration in AI. AI models like ChatGPT are trained on vast amounts of data. While OpenAI has made significant efforts to cleanse the training data to respect privacy, it is critical to ensure that ChatGPT is not used in a way that infringes on any privacy rights and laws. It is also important to note that, unless you have opted out, OpenAI may use chat data for further training of its models.

F. The Impact of AI on Jobs and the Economy

AI has the potential to significantly impact jobs and the economy, both positively and negatively. On one hand, AI can automate repetitive tasks, freeing up humans to focus on more complex and creative tasks, and even help create entirely new categories of jobs. On the other hand, the use of AI can transform current jobs, potentially leading to the replacement of certain roles and subsequent job displacement. For decision-makers, it is crucial to consider these impacts and focus on upskilling or reskilling employees, as their core skills may continue to add significant value to the business.

G. The Role of Regulation in AI Ethics

Regulation plays an important role in ensuring the ethical and fair use of technology, including AI. Governments and regulatory bodies around the world are working to develop regulations that ensure the responsible use of AI, protect individuals' rights, and prevent misuse while nurturing the innovation. As users of AI, it is important to stay informed about these regulations and ensure that our use of AI complies with them.

H. Additional Considerations

I will cover additional ethical and responsible use considerations in Section 3, which covers the integration of

ChatGPT with OpenAI APIs. In summary, while extending ChatGPT's capabilities through OpenAI APIs, web browsing, and plugins offers immense potential, it also introduces more complex ethical considerations. These complexities arise from dependencies on third parties and the need to manage user privacy, bias mitigation, transparency, factual accuracy, and even the possibility of unpredictable AI hallucinations.

Additionally, it is necessary to ensure the security of these integrations, obtain informed consent from users if their data is being used, establish clear lines of accountability, and ensure that these technologies are accessible to all. Lastly, the environmental impact of these technologies, due to their computational requirements, is another important consideration.

I. The Future of AI Ethics

As AI continues to evolve and become more integrated into our lives, the field of AI ethics will also continue to evolve. It is important to stay informed about the latest developments in AI ethics, and to continually reassess our use of AI to ensure that it remains ethical and responsible. This includes considering the potential long-term impacts of AI, striving to use it in a way that benefits all of society, and proactively mitigating any potential negative effects.

J. Summary

The exploration of AI, and particularly ChatGPT, brings with it a responsibility to use these powerful tools ethically and responsibly. As we venture deeper into AI's capabilities, it is critical to consider the potential impacts on individuals and society. By using ChatGPT responsibly and adhering to OpenAI's use-case policy, we can contribute to ensuring that it is used for the benefit of all.

In this chapter, we have discussed the importance of understanding AI ethics, the potential for misuse of AI, and the key role of transparency in AI. We have also underscored the significance of data privacy, the impact of AI on jobs and the economy, the role of regulation in maintaining AI ethics, and the continually evolving future of AI ethics. Additionally, we have highlighted the complexities that arise when integrating ChatGPT with third-party tools and the importance of considering security, consent, accountability, accessibility, and sustainability in these contexts.

The goal of AI is not to replace humans, but to augment our capabilities and make our lives better. It is up to us to use it wisely, ethically, safely, and responsibly.

SECTION 2: Using ChatGPT

A wide range of real-life examples

A Note on the Following Chapters

As we embark on this journey through the various applications of ChatGPT, it is important to set some expectations and provide a bit of context.

The chapters that follow are designed to demonstrate a wide range of real-life scenarios where ChatGPT can be applied. From day-to-day life and entrepreneurship to art and advanced topics, we will explore how this AI model can be a valuable tool in various contexts. However, these chapters merely scratch the surface of what is possible with ChatGPT. The potential applications are virtually limitless, and I encourage you to experiment and discover new uses beyond what is covered in this book.

I have used the simple, direct ChatGPT interface as a basis of examples within the scope of this book. However, once you start feeling comfortable with ChatGPT and writing effective prompts, I encourage you to experiment with the OpenAI Playground interface, which is described in detail in Section

1. This will enable you to generate more tailored responses without having to manage everything within your prompts.

As you develop expertise with ChatGPT, its Playground, and prompt engineering, you will find that the advanced topics of integrating and extending ChatGPT with the web, other applications, and plugins will open up a world of infinite possibilities

The content of this book is intended for educational and informational purposes. The interactions with ChatGPT presented in this book are fictitious examples, created to demonstrate its capabilities and potential uses. Any resemblance to real-life situations or existing content is purely coincidental and unintentional.

Lastly, to re-iterate, while I have striven to provide accurate and useful information in this educational book, you are ultimately responsible for any outcomes that may result from the use of the information contained within. AI, including ChatGPT, is a powerful tool, but it is not infallible. It is important to use it responsibly and ethically and to always double-check the information it provides, especially when making important decisions.

I hope that you find the following chapters enlightening and inspiring as you explore the possibilities of ChatGPT. Happy reading and experimenting!

7. ChatGPT for Day-To-Day Life

Life can be hectic. From managing your schedule to finding time for self-care, every day brings new challenges. Luckily, ChatGPT can be your personal assistant, helping you navigate through your daily tasks. This chapter will guide you with examples on using ChatGPT for day-to-day activities, making life a little bit easier.

A. Few Ideas and Examples

1. Scheduling and Task Management

ChatGPT can assist in prioritizing tasks, setting reminders, and managing your daily schedule.

Example: If you are trying to balance work tasks and personal errands, you could ask ChatGPT, "Help me prioritize my tasks for today. I have a project deadline, a grocery run, two meetings, and I need to pick up my kids from school.".

2. Cooking and Meal Planning

ChatGPT can help with recipe suggestions, meal planning, and even grocery shopping lists.

Example: If you want to cook a healthy dinner with chicken and broccoli, you could ask ChatGPT, "Give me a healthy recipe for a chicken and broccoli dinner.".

3. Fitness and Well-being

ChatGPT can provide workout suggestions, mindfulness exercises, and tips for healthier living.

Example: If you want to start a home workout routine, you might ask ChatGPT, "Suggest a beginner-friendly 30-minute home workout routine.”.

4. Learning and Personal Growth

ChatGPT can be a source of knowledge and learning. You can ask about historical events, scientific facts, or for book recommendations.

Example: If you are interested in learning about astronomy, you might ask ChatGPT, "Explain the basics of astronomy.”.

5. Other Examples

- Travel planning
- Home organization tips

- Parenting advice
- Mental health exercises
- Book recommendations

The possibilities are endless.

B. Applied Example: Meal Planning

Let's review a detailed interaction with ChatGPT for meal planning. Suppose you are trying to create a meal plan for the upcoming week. Here is how you might interact with ChatGPT:

User: I need to create a healthy meal plan for the next week. I'm a vegetarian and I'm trying to include more protein in my diet. Can you help me with that?

ChatGPT: Absolutely! Here's a simple meal plan you could consider:

Monday

- **Breakfast**: Greek yogurt with mixed berries and a sprinkle of granola.

- **Lunch**: Quinoa salad with chickpeas, cucumber, cherry tomatoes, and feta.

- **Dinner**: Lentil curry with brown rice.

Tuesday

```
  - **Breakfast**: Scrambled tofu with whole grain toast and avocado.

  - **Lunch**: Vegetable stir-fry with tempeh and brown rice.

  - **Dinner**: Stuffed bell peppers with black beans and quinoa.
```

The conversation could then continue, with ChatGPT creating a meal plan for the rest of the week, and even generating a grocery list if needed.

C. Exercises

Write prompts asking ChatGPT:
• To help prioritize your tasks for the day.
• For a home workout routine.
• To explain a topic that you are interested in.
• For suggestions on how to handle a difficult conversation.
• For a step-by-step guide on how to perform a specific task, like fixing a common household item.

D. Summary

ChatGPT can be your personal assistant, helping you with a myriad of day-to-day tasks. From managing your schedule to fostering personal growth, ChatGPT can help make life easier.

8. ChatGPT for Home

Life at home, whether you are a working professional, a homemaker, or a retiree, can be filled with a multitude of tasks, from planning meals and organizing chores to helping children with homework and managing personal finances. While these tasks are essential, they can often be time-consuming. This is where AI, particularly ChatGPT, can step in as an incredibly useful tool, providing assistance and automation in various home tasks, enhancing efficiency, and freeing up time for other activities. This chapter explores some practical examples of how to utilize the capabilities of ChatGPT to simplify life at home.

A. Few Ideas and Examples

1. Planning and Organizing Chores

ChatGPT can assist in creating schedules and chore charts for efficient task management at home. Based on the number of family members, their respective duties, and the frequency of chores, you can interact with ChatGPT to create a well-structured plan.

Example: Suppose you have a family of four, and you want to divide chores equally among all members. You could ask ChatGPT, "Create a weekly chore schedule for a family of four.". ChatGPT can then generate a balanced chore chart assigning different tasks to each member on different days.

2. Assisting with DIY Projects

From crafting to home improvement, ChatGPT can provide step-by-step instructions, tips, and even safety measures for various DIY (Do It Yourself) projects based on its extensive knowledge base.

Example: If you are interested in building a birdhouse but don't know where to start, you could prompt ChatGPT with something like, "Provide step-by-step instructions to build a simple birdhouse.".

3. Creating Shopping Lists

Whether it is for groceries or a special event, ChatGPT can aid in drafting detailed shopping lists. By providing it with basic information such as the type of event or your regular eating habits, ChatGPT can suggest an appropriate list of items to purchase.

Example: For instance, if you are planning a BBQ party for ten people, you might ask ChatGPT, "Create a shopping list for a BBQ party for ten people.". ChatGPT could then generate a list including items like various meats, BBQ sauce, charcoal, paper plates, and more.

4. Providing Recipes

ChatGPT can be your personal digital chef, offering recipes based on the ingredients you have at hand, your dietary restrictions, or the type of meal you want to prepare.

Example: You could ask ChatGPT, "What is a quick dinner recipe I can make with chicken, broccoli, and rice?". Based on these ingredients, it can provide a simple recipe for you to follow.

5. Assisting with Homework or Tutoring Kids

ChatGPT can be a valuable educational tool, providing explanations for complex concepts, offering solutions for mathematical problems, and even assisting with language learning and reading comprehension.

Example: If your child needs help with a math problem, you could input the problem into ChatGPT. For instance, "Help solve this math problem: A train moving at 60 miles per hour takes 1.5 hours to reach its destination. How far did it travel?". ChatGPT can provide a step-by-step solution, explaining how it arrived at the answer.

6. Planning Home Decor or Renovations

ChatGPT can offer ideas and advice on home decor or renovation projects based on your preferences and budget. It can suggest color schemes, furniture arrangement, and even where to source materials.

Example: If you are planning to redecorate your living room with a mid-century modern aesthetic, you could ask ChatGPT, "What are some key elements and color schemes in mid-century modern decor for my living room?". ChatGPT could then provide a list of key elements to consider and suggest color schemes that align with that style.

7. Other Examples

- Home Maintenance
- Gardening
- Entertainment
- Home fitness
- Home Remedies

The possibilities are endless.

B. Applied Example: Help with an Assignment

Here is a detailed simulation of how a user might interact with ChatGPT to assist a child with a history assignment.

Let's say your child needs to write a short report about the Civil War. They are having trouble understanding the causes of the war. Here is how you might interact with ChatGPT:

User: My 12 year old child needs to write a report on the Civil War. Can you explain the main causes of the Civil War in a simple and concise manner?

ChatGPT: Of course! Here's a simple explanation:

The Civil War had several key causes:

1. **Slavery**: This was the major cause. The southern states, also known as the Confederacy, wanted to maintain slavery as it was crucial for their agricultural economy. The northern states, the Union, however, were moving towards industrialization and wanted to end slavery.

2. **Economic Differences**: The North was industrialized and the South was agricultural. These differing economies led to disagreements on issues such as taxes and tariffs.

3. **States' Rights vs. Federal Rights**: The Southern states believed that they had the right to make their own decisions, such as keeping slavery, without federal government intervention.

4. **The Election of Abraham Lincoln**: Lincoln was against the expansion of slavery into new territories, which upset the southern states and was a factor that led to the war.

```
Remember, these are complex issues and this is a simplified explanation for a child. A more detailed examination would include the nuances and complexities of these causes.
```

This example demonstrates how ChatGPT can simplify complex subjects for children. It is also a great tool for parents who may need a refresher on certain subjects in order to assist their children with homework.

C. Exercises

Write prompts asking ChatGPT:
• To create a chore schedule for your family.
• For a simple explanation of a complex concept for a child.
• For ideas to redecorate a room in your house.
• For tips on how to care for a specific type of houseplant.
• To create a checklist of regular home maintenance tasks, or how to perform simple home repairs.

D. Summary

In this chapter, we have explored various ways in which ChatGPT can assist with daily tasks at home, from planning chores and DIY projects to tutoring children and planning home decor. The potential uses of ChatGPT at home are vast and varied. It is all about learning to ask the right questions to get the most out of this powerful AI tool.

9. ChatGPT for Work

In today's digital age, AI tools like ChatGPT are revolutionizing the way we work. Whether you are a professional in a large corporation, a freelancer, or a remote worker, ChatGPT can be a valuable assistant, helping you streamline tasks and boost productivity. This chapter will explore how you can leverage ChatGPT in various work scenarios.

However, it's important to remember that all interactions with ChatGPT should align with your employer's policies and guidelines. Be sure to review and understand your workplace's policy on AI use before integrating ChatGPT into your daily work processes.

A. Few Ideas and Examples

1. Task Management

ChatGPT can assist you in prioritizing your work tasks, setting reminders, and helping you stay organized.

Example: If you are feeling overwhelmed with your to-do list, you could ask ChatGPT, "How can I effectively prioritize my tasks for the day? Here are some of my tasks…."

2. Communication

ChatGPT can help draft, proofread, and refine your professional emails, messages, reports, and presentations.

Example: If you are drafting a report on your project's progress, you could ask ChatGPT, "Help me write a progress report on my project about implementing AI solutions in our customer service operations. Here are some details about the project…".

3. Decision Making

ChatGPT can provide you with data-driven insights, helping you make informed decisions. You could ask it for advantages and disadvantages, pros and cons, or to play devil's advocate on certain topics.

Example: If you are considering a shift to remote work, you could ask ChatGPT, "What are the pros and cons of shifting to a remote work model?".

4. Professional Development

ChatGPT can assist you in your professional growth by providing insights into industry trends, helping you prepare for interviews, or suggesting resources for learning new skills.

Example: If you are a marketing professional looking to enhance your skills, you could ask ChatGPT, "What are the top digital marketing strategies I should be aware of?".

5. Other Examples

- Ideas for projects
- Job interview preparation
- Drafting proposals
- Writing LinkedIn profiles
- Meeting agenda planning

The possibilities are endless.

B. Applied Example: Communication

Let's look at a detailed simulation of how an individual might use ChatGPT for professional communication. Suppose you need to send an email to a colleague asking them for their inputs on a document you are working on. Here is how you might interact with ChatGPT:

User: I need to write an email to my colleague, John, asking for his feedback on the marketing proposal I've been working on. Can you help me draft this email?

ChatGPT: Sure, here's a suggestion:

Subject: Request for Feedback on Marketing Proposal

Hi John,

I hope this email finds you well. I've been working on our new marketing proposal and have put together a draft that I believe captures our objectives well.

However, your insights, especially concerning our SEO strategy, would be invaluable. Could you take some time to review the document and provide your feedback? I am particularly interested in your thoughts on the keyword strategy and content marketing plan.

I've attached the proposal to this email. Let's aim to finalize the document by the end of this week, if possible.

Looking forward to your expert feedback.

Best Regards,

[Your Name]

User: That's great. Can we also set up a meeting to discuss his feedback?

ChatGPT: Absolutely, here's the revised version:

Subject: Request for Feedback and Meeting on Marketing Proposal

Hi John,

```
I hope this email finds you well. I've been working on our new marketing proposal and have drafted a preliminary document. Your insights, especially concerning our SEO strategy, would be invaluable, and I'd like to request your feedback.

In addition to your written feedback, it would be great if we could set up a meeting to discuss your thoughts in more depth. This collaborative approach will ensure we produce the most effective strategy possible. How does your schedule look this week for a brief meeting?

I've attached the proposal to this email.

Looking forward to your feedback and our discussion.


Best Regards,

[Your Name]
```

In this example, you can see how ChatGPT can help draft professional, polite, and effective emails. It is essential to provide specific details about what you need to get the most appropriate response.

C. Exercises

Write prompts asking ChatGPT:
• To help prioritize your tasks for the day.

Write prompts asking ChatGPT:
• To draft an email to a colleague.
• For the pros and cons of a particular decision at work.
• For information on tools in your professional field.
• Summarize meetings minutes

D. Summary

ChatGPT can be an invaluable tool in a professional setting. From managing tasks and drafting communications to aiding in decision making and professional development, ChatGPT can help make your workday more productive. Your interactions with ChatGPT should align with your employer's policies and guidelines on workplace AI use.

10. ChatGPT for Business

In a world that is increasingly reliant on digital solutions, businesses are turning to AI tools to enhance their operations, improve decision-making processes, and drive growth. Language models like ChatGPT can be instrumental in various business applications, from internal communications and HR functions to sales, marketing, and customer service. In this chapter, we will look into examples on how businesses can leverage the power of ChatGPT.

It is important to remember that the implementation and use of AI tools like ChatGPT should always comply with a company's policies and guidelines, as well as local and international regulations. As we explore examples of how businesses can leverage the power of ChatGPT in this chapter, remember to consider these policy and legal considerations.

A. Few Ideas and Examples

1. Internal Communications

ChatGPT can help generate, proofread, and refine company-wide communications, emails, presentations, or meeting agendas.

Example: If you are drafting an email to your team about an upcoming meeting, you might ask ChatGPT, "Help me write an email to my team regarding an upcoming strategic planning meeting.".

2. Human Resources (HR)

ChatGPT can assist in drafting job descriptions, refining employee surveys, or creating training materials.

Example: If you are an HR professional looking to create a new job description for a digital marketing role, you might ask ChatGPT, "Write a job description for a Digital Marketing Specialist position in my company.".

3. Sales and Customer Acquisition

ChatGPT can generate sales scripts, help respond to common customer queries, or craft personalized sales pitches.

Example: If you are a sales representative and want assistance with a sales script, you might ask ChatGPT, "Can you help me draft a sales script for our new line of eco-friendly beauty products?".

4. Marketing and Advertising

ChatGPT can generate marketing copy, suggest promotional strategies, or create compelling content for your social media channels.

Example: If you are looking to promote a new service your business is offering, you might ask ChatGPT, "Help me draft a Facebook post announcing the launch of our new personal finance consulting service.".

5. Customer Service

ChatGPT can be integrated into customer service operations to respond to customer inquiries, provide product information, or troubleshoot common issues.

Example: If you are setting up a chatbot for your online store, you could have ChatGPT respond to common inquiries, such as "What are the shipping options?".

6. Other Examples

- Competitor analysis
- Product research and descriptions
- Crisis management scripts
- Influencer outreach
- Analyzing sales trends

The possibilities are endless.

B. Applied Example: Sales and Customer Acquisition

Here is a detailed simulation of how a business might use ChatGPT for sales and customer acquisition. Let is say you are a sales manager for a tech startup that offers a project management tool, and you are reaching out to potential customers via email. Here is how you might interact with ChatGPT:

User: I need to write a persuasive sales email to potential customers for our new project management tool, which helps teams collaborate effectively and complete projects faster. Can you help me craft this email?

ChatGPT: Absolutely! Here's a suggestion:

Subject: Revolutionize Your Team's Collaboration with [Your Tool's Name]

Dear [Customer's Name],

I hope this message finds you well. My name is [Your Name] and I represent [Your Startup's Name], a tech startup focused on transforming the way teams collaborate and achieve their project goals.

We understand the challenges that come with managing a team and ensuring everyone is aligned, which is why we've developed [Your Tool's Name], a state-of-the-art project management tool designed to boost productivity and streamline team collaboration.

With [Your Tool's Name], you can expect:

- Easy-to-use features for task assignment, progress tracking, and communication.
- Increased efficiency as team members can prioritize tasks and meet deadlines.
- Real-time updates, ensuring everyone is on the same page, reducing misunderstandings and repeated work.

We would be thrilled to offer you a free trial, demonstrating how [Your Tool's Name] can revolutionize your project management and significantly impact your team's productivity.

Looking forward to hearing from you.

Best Regards,

[Your Name]

User: That's great! But I'd like to add a personalized touch based on the potential customer's industry, which is construction.

ChatGPT: Absolutely! Here's an updated version:

Subject: Revolutionize Your Construction Project Management with [Your Tool's Name]

Dear [Customer's Name],

As someone who is deeply involved in the construction industry, you understand better than anyone the importance of seamless collaboration and efficient project management. At [Your Startup's Name], we've developed a solution that caters specifically to these needs.

[Your Tool's Name] is not just any project management tool; it's designed with industries like construction in mind. Features like robust task assignment, real-time updates, and progress tracking are tailored to handle the dynamic and complex tasks that construction projects entail.

Imagine a platform where you can see the progress of each project phase, delegate tasks based on expertise, and ensure everyone is updated with the most recent project changes. That's what [Your Tool's Name] delivers.

We would be thrilled to offer you a free trial so you can see firsthand how [Your Tool's Name] can revolutionize your project management and significantly enhance your construction projects' efficiency.

Looking forward to hearing from you.

Best Regards,

[Your Name]

This example illustrates how ChatGPT can generate industry-specific, personalized sales pitches. Providing more detailed information in your prompts will result in more tailored outputs.

C. Exercises

Write prompts asking ChatGPT:
• To help draft a company-wide email.
• To help create a job description.
• To help craft a sales script.
• To analyze a sales report.
• To respond to a common customer inquiry.

D. Summary

ChatGPT can be a transformative tool for businesses across various departments. From HR and internal communications to sales, marketing, and customer service, ChatGPT can automate and refine many tasks, allowing businesses to save time and focus on strategy and growth. The possibilities are nearly endless, and with the right prompts while adhering to regulations and your business's policies and guidelines, ChatGPT can become a powerful assistant in your business operations.

11. ChatGPT for Finance

Financial management and investing involve complex decision-making processes based on the analysis of large amounts of data. By leveraging the capabilities of AI tools such as ChatGPT, finance professionals and individual investors can make more informed decisions.

This chapter provides a guide on how to use ChatGPT for various financial tasks including financial analysis, investment advice, market predictions, and report generation.

A. Few Ideas and Examples

1. Financial Analysis

ChatGPT can be used to assist in financial analysis. By feeding it relevant data or context, you can ask it to summarize financial reports, or generate simplified explanations of complex financial statements.

Example: You might prompt ChatGPT with, "Explain the key points from this annual financial report of XYZ Corporation.". ChatGPT could then generate a simplified summary, highlighting data points like profits, losses, assets, liabilities, and overall financial health.

2. General Investment Advice

ChatGPT can provide generic investment advice based on broad market knowledge. It can generate a list of investment strategies, or advise on risk management based on theoretical information. It is essential to remember that ChatGPT does not have real-time market data or specific professional expertise, and its advice should always be cross-verified.

Example: You could ask ChatGPT, "What are some general strategies for investing in a volatile stock market?". ChatGPT might suggest strategies like diversifying your portfolio, prioritizing blue-chip stocks, or investing in sectors that tend to do well during market downturns.

3. Assessing Market Trends

While ChatGPT cannot predict market trends due to its inability to process real-time data and its lack of professional financial expertise, it can explain the factors that often influence market trends based on its training data.

Example: You might ask ChatGPT, "What are some factors that could affect the stock market?". ChatGPT could provide a list of factors such as economic indicators, interest rates, political stability, and more.

4. Report Generation

ChatGPT can assist in drafting financial reports or documents. It can provide outlines, suggest key points to include, and even generate sections of the report.

Example: If you are drafting a report on the financial performance of a company, you might ask ChatGPT, "What are the key points to include in a financial performance report for XYZ Corporation?" ChatGPT could provide a list of points to consider, such as revenue, net income, operating costs, assets and liabilities, and cash flow.

5. Other Examples

- Explaining financial jargon.
- Generating customer service frequently asked questions FAQs for financial services
- Drafting investment portfolios
- Financial education and tutoring
- Assisting in year-end financial preparation

The possibilities are limitless.

B. Applied Example: Financial Analysis

Here is a simulated example of how a user might interact with ChatGPT to perform financial analysis. Let's assume you are reviewing earnings report of XYZ Company and need help interpreting it.

```
User: I would like some analysis based on these figures:

Balance Sheet for the Fiscal Year Ended 2022

Cash: $2,000,000
Accounts Receivable: $1,500,000
Inventory: $500,000
Property, Plant, and Equipment: $10,000,000
Total Assets: $14,000,000
Accounts Payable: $1,200,000
Long-term Debt: $6,000,000
Total Liabilities: $7,200,000
Common Stock: $1,000,000
Retained Earnings: $5,800,000
Total Equity: $6,800,000


Income Statement for the Fiscal Year Ended 2022

Revenue: $10,000,000
Cost of Goods Sold: $3,000,000
Gross Profit: $7,000,000
```

Operating Expenses: $4,500,000

Operating Income: $2,500,000

Interest Expense: $400,000

Taxes: $500,000

Net Income: $1,600,000

Could you give me an analysis of liquidity, profitability, and leverage?

ChatGPT: Based on the provided financials, here's a basic analysis:

Liquidity:

The current ratio (Current Assets / Current Liabilities) is 2.92 (($2,000,000 Cash + $1,500,000 Accounts Receivable) / $1,200,000 Accounts Payable). This ratio suggests that the company has more than enough short-term assets to cover its short-term liabilities.

Profitability:

The net profit margin (Net Income / Revenue) is 16% ($1,600,000 / $10,000,000). This suggests that 16% of each dollar in revenue is actual profit, which is a relatively healthy profitability ratio.

The gross profit margin (Gross Profit / Revenue) is 70% ($7,000,000 / $10,000,000), which suggests that the company makes 70 cents of gross profit for each dollar of revenue.

Leverage:

The debt-to-equity ratio (Total Liabilities / Total Equity) is 1.06 ($7,200,000 / $6,800,000). This implies the company is moderately leveraged,

```
using about as much debt as equity to finance its
assets.

  Remember, this is a simplified analysis and
further investigation might be necessary to
understand the complete financial condition.
```

C. Exercises

Write prompts asking ChatGPT:
• To summarize a financial report of your choice.
• To suggest general strategies for investing in real estate.
• To explain factors that might affect the cryptocurrency market.
• For key points to include in a financial performance report for a specific company.
• To interpret and compare financial metrics from different companies.

D. Summary

In this chapter, we have explored various applications of ChatGPT in the financial domain. From assisting in financial analysis to providing investment advice, understanding market influences, and aiding in report generation, ChatGPT can be a valuable tool for finance professionals and individual investors. However, it's crucial to remember that the advice and outputs generated by ChatGPT are based on theoretical knowledge and historical data and should always be cross-verified with real-time data or professional advice.

12. ChatGPT for Entrepreneurs

Entrepreneurship is filled with challenges and opportunities. In this digital age, AI has become a valuable tool for entrepreneurs, providing assistance in various tasks and decision-making processes. From idea generation and marketing to business planning and networking, AI can provide valuable insights and automate tasks, freeing up entrepreneurs to focus on strategic decision-making

This chapter will guide you with some relevant examples on how to leverage the power of AI to brainstorm business ideas, enhance your marketing efforts, plan your business, and foster effective networking and collaboration.

A. Few Ideas and Examples

1. Idea Generation

ChatGPT can be a valuable tool for brainstorming business ideas. By providing it with a seed idea or a set of parameters, it can generate a list of potential business ideas. It can also help in validating and refining these ideas.

Example: Suppose you are interested in starting a business in the sustainable fashion industry. You might prompt ChatGPT with something like, "Generate a list of innovative business ideas for the sustainable fashion industry.". ChatGPT could then provide a list of potential business ideas, such as a clothing line that uses recycled materials, an online platform for swapping high-quality used clothing, or a service that helps fashion brands audit their supply chains for sustainability.

You can also ask ChatGPT to provide feedback on your ideas, helping you to refine and improve them.

2. Marketing and Advertising

ChatGPT can assist in creating compelling copy for your marketing and advertising campaigns. It can generate content for social media posts, ad copies, blog posts, and more. It can also help in strategizing your social media presence.

Example: If you are running a local bakery and want to create a social media post to promote a new type of pastry, you could ask ChatGPT, "Write a catchy social media post to promote a new chocolate croissant at a local bakery.". ChatGPT might generate something like, "Craving something sweet and flaky? Our new chocolate croissants are fresh out of the oven! Stop by today to enjoy this buttery delight filled with rich, melted chocolate. #LocalBakery #FreshPastries #ChocolateLovers"

3. Business Planning

ChatGPT can aid in drafting business plans and proposals. It can provide outlines, suggest key points to include, and even generate sections of the plan. It can also assist in financial projections and analysis.

Example: If you are drafting a business plan for a tech startup, you might ask ChatGPT, "What are the key points to include in a business plan for a tech startup?". ChatGPT could provide a list of points to consider, such as executive summary, company description, market analysis, organization and management structure, service or product line, marketing and sales strategy, funding request, financial projections, and an appendix.

4. Networking and Collaboration

ChatGPT can help find potential partners and resources by generating a list of possible contacts or platforms to explore. It can also assist in communication strategies and negotiation tactics.

Example: If you are looking to connect with other entrepreneurs in the sustainable fashion industry, you could ask ChatGPT, "What are some strategies for networking with other entrepreneurs in the sustainable fashion industry?". ChatGPT might suggest attending industry-specific events or conferences, joining online forums or social media groups related to sustainable fashion, or reaching out directly to individuals whose work you admire.

5. Other Examples

- New product or service ideas.
- Creating business pitch decks.
- Creating term sheets or other such documents.
- Automating routine business reports.
- Role playing for an upcoming venture capital pitch.

The possibilities are endless.

B. Applied Example: Marketing and Advertising

Here is a detailed simulation of how a user might interact with ChatGPT to create a social media post for a new product.

Let's say you are launching a new eco-friendly water bottle under your brand, "ProtoHydrate". You want to create a compelling social media post to announce the product launch. Here is how you might interact with ChatGPT:

User: I need to create a social media post for the launch of our new eco-friendly water bottle. The bottle is made from 100% recycled materials, keeps liquids cold for up to 24 hours, and a tree is planted for every bottle sold. Our brand, ProtoHydrate, is all about promoting sustainable living and hydration. Can you help me craft a catchy and engaging post?

ChatGPT: Absolutely! Here's a suggestion:

🌍 Meet the newest member of the ProtoHydrate family - our Eco-Friendly Water Bottle! 💧 Not only does it keep your drinks cold for up to 24 hours, but it's also made from 100% recycled materials. But that's not all - for every bottle sold, we're planting a tree! 🌳 Stay hydrated, help the planet, and join us in promoting a sustainable lifestyle with ProtoHydrate. #ProtoHydrate #SustainableLiving #StayHydrated

User: That's great! Can we also mention that it's perfect for summer adventures?

ChatGPT: Of course! Here's the updated post:

🌍 Say hello to your perfect summer companion - the new Eco-Friendly Water Bottle from ProtoHydrate! 💧 Made from 100% recycled materials, it keeps your drinks icy cold for up to 24 hours, making it ideal for all your summer adventures. 🌞 And the best part? For every bottle sold, we're planting a tree! 🌳 Join us in promoting sustainable living and stay hydrated

```
with ProtoHydrate. #SustainableLiving
#ProtoHydrate #SummerAdventures #EcoFriendly.
```

This example demonstrates how you can interact with ChatGPT iteratively, refining the output until you get the desired result. It is important to provide as much relevant information as possible in your prompts and to be specific about what you are asking for.

This is just one example of how you can use ChatGPT for marketing and advertising. Feel free to experiment with different prompts and scenarios to see what works best for your specific needs.

C. Exercises

Write a prompt asking ChatGPT:
• To generate a list of business ideas for a specific industry of your choice.
• To create a social media post promoting a product or service.
• For the key points to include in a business plan for a specific type of business.
• For strategies for networking in a specific industry.
• To create a presentation based on some detailed content you provide. Provide specific instructions on what you

Write a prompt asking ChatGPT:

would like to achieve from the presentation and who your audience is.

D. Summary

In this chapter, we have explored the various ways ChatGPT can assist entrepreneurs. From generating innovative business ideas and crafting compelling marketing copy, to aiding in business planning and networking strategies, ChatGPT can be a valuable tool for entrepreneurs.

13. ChatGPT for eCommerce

In the ever-evolving world of eCommerce, staying ahead of the competition can be a daunting task. As an online retailer or an eCommerce entrepreneur, maintaining an online store, managing inventory, handling customer queries, and marketing products can be quite the juggling act. AI, particularly language models like ChatGPT, can assist in these various tasks related to eCommerce, offering significant enhancements in efficiency and customer experience. This chapter will detail how you can leverage ChatGPT for your eCommerce business.

You can even integrate ChatGPT in your eCommerce site directly to create a chatbot or other such self-services for customers. This is an advanced topic beyond the scope for this book. However, please see Section 3 for an overview on ChatGPT APIs which can get you started.

A. Few Ideas and Examples

1. Product Description Generation

ChatGPT can help in writing persuasive, unique, and SEO (Search Engine Optimization)-friendly product descriptions.

Example: Suppose you sell handmade candles and need a captivating description for a new lavender-scented candle. You could ask ChatGPT, "Write a product description for a lavender-scented, handmade candle. The product name is…".

2. Customer Support

ChatGPT can act as the first line of customer support, answering common queries, providing information on shipping and returns, and even guiding customers on product usage.

Example: Customers often have questions about product usage. For example, if you sell electronic gadgets, customers might need help with setting up or troubleshooting. You could use ChatGPT to provide step-by-step guides or to answer common questions.

If you want to prepare responses for common customer inquiries, you might ask ChatGPT, "Draft a polite and informative response to a customer asking about the shipping status of their order.".

3. Personalized Product Recommendations

ChatGPT can suggest products to customers based on their interests, shopping history, or queries. This can enhance the shopping experience and increase the likelihood of purchases.

Example: If a customer is looking for camping gear, you could use ChatGPT to recommend relevant products. You might ask it, "Generate a list of recommended camping gear products for a customer planning a summer camping trip.".

4. Review Analysis

ChatGPT can analyze product reviews, providing summaries of customer feedback, identifying common complaints, and even suggesting potential improvements.

Example: If you sell kitchen appliances and you have a product with mixed reviews, you could ask ChatGPT, "Analyze and summarize customer reviews for Product X. Here is a sample set of reviews: ...". This could help you understand customer needs and improve your products.

5. Social Media and Email Marketing

ChatGPT can assist in creating engaging social media posts, newsletters, and email campaigns, helping to attract and retain customers.

Example: If you are running a seasonal sale and want to announce it on social media, you could ask ChatGPT, "Write a catchy social media post announcing a summer sale for our online clothing store.".

6. Other Examples

- Pricing strategies.
- Language translations for Blogs.
- Ideas for sales promotions or events.
- User guides or FAQs for products.
- SEO-friendly product blog posts or articles.

The possibilities are endless.

B. Applied Example: Product Description Generation

Let's dive into a detailed simulation of how you might use ChatGPT to strategize a marketing campaign for your eCommerce store. Suppose you are launching a new line of organic skincare products. Here is how you might interact with ChatGPT:

User: I'm launching a new line of organic skincare products in my online store. I need to create a comprehensive marketing campaign. Can you help me brainstorm some ideas?

ChatGPT: Absolutely! Here are a few marketing strategies you could consider:

1. **Content Marketing**: Share blog posts or articles about the benefits of organic skincare, ingredients used in your products, or skincare routines using your products.

2. **Social Media Campaign**: Launch a social media campaign introducing the new product line. Use engaging visuals and short videos demonstrating the products.

3. **Influencer Marketing**: Collaborate with influencers who align with your brand values to reach a larger audience.

4. **Email Marketing**: Send an email blast to your subscribers announcing the launch, perhaps offering a discount code for their first purchase from the new line.

5. **Customer Reviews**: Encourage customers to review the new products and share their experiences on your website or social media.

User: That's a great start. Can you help me write a blog post on the benefits of organic skincare?

ChatGPT: Certainly! Here's a draft introduction for your blog post:

Title: Unlock the Power of Nature: The Benefits of Organic Skincare

In a world full of synthetic beauty solutions, choosing organic skincare products is like taking a rejuvenating breath of fresh air. Organic skincare, untainted by harsh chemicals,

```
prioritizes the natural balance of your skin, harnessing the healing and nurturing properties of Mother Nature herself. In this article, we'll explore the undeniable benefits of choosing organic skincare products and why they should be part of your daily beauty regimen...
```

Here is a detailed simulation of how you might interact with ChatGPT to create a product description. Let's say you are selling a new line of vegan, cruelty-free lipsticks and you need a compelling product description. Here is how you might interact with ChatGPT:

> **User**: I need a captivating product description for our new line of vegan, cruelty-free lipsticks. The lipsticks come in a range of ten colors, have a smooth, hydrating formula, and are packaged in recyclable materials. Can you help me write a product description?
>
> **ChatGPT**: Absolutely! Here's a suggestion:
>
> Introducing our vibrant new line of vegan, cruelty-free lipsticks! Crafted with love and conscious responsibility, each lipstick boasts a palette of ten stunning colors that glide on smoothly for a rich, hydrating finish. Not only will your lips look lush and lovely, but you can also feel-good knowing that our lipsticks are 100% vegan and cruelty-free. Plus, they come packaged in eco-friendly, recyclable materials. Treat your lips to the care they deserve and make an environmentally friendly choice with our beautiful new range.

This example shows how you can interact with ChatGPT to generate engaging and informative product descriptions. Specificity in your prompts will often yield better results.

C. Exercises

Write prompts asking ChatGPT:
• To generate a product description for an item of your choice.
• For personalized product recommendations based on a customer's interests.
• To analyze customer reviews for a specific product.
• To create a social media post or email newsletter promoting your online store or a specific product.
• To analyze the sales of a particular product in your store

D. Summary

In this chapter, we have reviewed various ways in which ChatGPT can assist with eCommerce, from product descriptions and customer support to personalized recommendations and marketing. Whether you are running a large online store or a small online boutique, ChatGPT can be a valuable addition to your business, increasing efficiency and enhancing customer experiences.

14. ChatGPT for Service Industry

The service industry is a broad and diverse sector that includes areas like hospitality, travel, healthcare, professional services, and more. Efficient communication, customer service, and strategic planning are vital elements of this industry. ChatGPT can assist in all these areas, enhancing efficiency, and improving customer satisfaction.

A. Few Ideas and Examples

1. Customer Communication

ChatGPT can be utilized to automate responses to frequent customer queries or draft personalized responses.

Example: If you run a hotel and receive a common query such as "What amenities are included in my booking?". You could ask ChatGPT, "Draft a response detailing the amenities included in a standard hotel room booking.".

2. Marketing and Advertising

ChatGPT can assist in creating engaging content for your marketing and advertising campaigns, from drafting social media posts to creating compelling descriptions of your services.

Example: If you own a travel agency and want to promote a new travel package, you might ask ChatGPT, "Write a compelling description for a new luxury cruise package. Here are some specifics…".

3. Service Improvement and Planning

ChatGPT can assist in identifying areas of service improvement, generating new service ideas, or devising strategic service delivery plans.

Example: If you are looking to enhance the guest experience in your restaurant, you could ask ChatGPT, "Generate a list of ideas to improve the dining experience in a fine dining restaurant.".

4. Staff Training

ChatGPT can help in creating training content, role-playing scenarios, or explaining industry-specific concepts to the staff.

Example: If you are training hotel staff to handle guest complaints, you might ask ChatGPT, "Create a role-playing scenario where a hotel staff member efficiently resolves a guest complaint about room service.".

5. Other Examples

- Service feedback responses
- Crisis communication
- Service pricing strategy
- Service Confirmation emails
- Service outage planning

The possibilities are endless.

B. Applied Example: Marketing and Advertising

Let's look at a detailed interaction with ChatGPT where it assists in creating marketing content for a new service. Suppose you are launching a new spa service at your wellness center. Here is how you might interact with ChatGPT:

```
User: I am launching a new holistic spa service at my wellness center which includes aromatherapy, a full-body massage, and a detox sauna session. I want to create an appealing social media post to attract our target audience. Can you help?

ChatGPT: Of course! Here's a suggestion:

Immerse yourself in ultimate relaxation with our new holistic spa service! 🌿 Breathe in tranquility with our soothing aromatherapy, let
```

```
our expert therapists melt away your stress with a full-body massage, and end your session with a cleansing detox sauna. 🧖‍♀️ Escape the everyday and rejuvenate your senses at our wellness center. Book your spot today! #WellnessJourney #HolisticSpa #RelaxandRenew
```

C. Exercises

Write prompts asking ChatGPT:
• To respond to a common customer query.
• To create a social media post for a new service.
• For ideas to improve a specific service.
• To create a staff training scenario.
• For ideas on enhancing service for a certain holiday.

D. Summary

ChatGPT can be a valuable tool for the service industry, enhancing customer communication, aiding in service planning, generating compelling marketing content, and assisting with staff training. The key is to provide clear and detailed prompts to get the most relevant responses.

15. ChatGPT for Manufacturing

Manufacturing is a complex sector that involves various stages from planning and designing to production and quality control. ChatGPT can assist in each of these stages, making the process more efficient and streamlined.

A. Few Ideas and Examples

1. Idea Generation and Design

ChatGPT can aid in brainstorming ideas for new products or improvements in existing designs. It can also help in creating detailed product descriptions or specifications.

Example: If you are in the business of manufacturing sports equipment and want to design a new type of running shoe, you could ask ChatGPT, "Generate a list of innovative features for a new running shoe.".

2. Process Planning

ChatGPT can assist in creating a detailed manufacturing process plan, outlining the steps involved, the resources required, and potential challenges.

Example: If you are planning to manufacture a smartphone, you might ask ChatGPT, "Outline the manufacturing process for a smartphone.”.

3. Quality Control

ChatGPT can help in creating quality control checklists, outlining standards for different processes, and suggesting improvements.

Example: If you want to ensure the quality of your production process, you could ask ChatGPT, "Generate a quality control checklist for the production of laptop computers.”.

4. Troubleshooting and Problem-Solving

ChatGPT can assist in identifying solutions to common manufacturing problems or suggest ways to troubleshoot issues.

Example: If you are facing issues with the efficiency of your assembly line, you could ask ChatGPT, "Suggest ways to improve the efficiency of an assembly line.”.

5. Other Examples

- Product cost estimation
- Inventory management
- Production scheduling
- Maintenance planning
- Capacity planning

The possibilities are endless.

B. Applied Example: Process Planning

Let's examine a detailed example of how a user might interact with ChatGPT to plan a manufacturing process. Suppose you are considering producing a new type of eco-friendly reusable water bottle. Here is how you might interact with ChatGPT:

User: I'm planning to manufacture an eco-friendly reusable water bottle made from plant-based plastics. Can you outline the manufacturing process steps, resources required, and potential challenges?

ChatGPT: Sure, here is a basic outline:

1. **Concept and Design**: Your process should start with concept and design, creating precise specifications and blueprints for the water bottle.

2. **Material Acquisition**: For the plant-based plastics, you would need to source materials like

corn starch, PLA pellets, and biodegradable additives.

3. **Injection Molding**: The plant-based plastic pellets will be melted and injected into a mold of the water bottle.

4. **Cooling and Removal**: The mold will need to be cooled before the newly-formed bottles can be removed.

5. **Post-Processing**: Any necessary post-processing, such as removing excess plastic and checking for defects, will take place.

6. **Assembly**: If the bottle has multiple parts (like a cap), these will need to be assembled.

7. **Quality Control**: The bottles will undergo a thorough quality check to ensure they meet your standards.

8. **Packaging**: The bottles are then packaged, ready for distribution.

Resources required would include manufacturing machinery such as an injection molding machine, materials for the bottle, quality control instruments, and manpower.

Potential challenges could include sourcing high-quality plant-based plastics, ensuring the product is durable despite being eco-friendly, and maintaining a manufacturing process that is as eco-friendly as the product itself.

C. Exercises

Write prompts asking ChatGPT:
• To generate ideas for a new product.
• To outline a manufacturing process.
• To create a quality control checklist.
• For troubleshooting solutions to a manufacturing issue.
• For a job description for a shift supervisor

D. Summary

ChatGPT can prove to be a useful tool in the manufacturing sector, assisting in the ideation and design phase, process planning, quality control, and troubleshooting. The key is to provide clear and detailed prompts fine-tuned to your scenarios to get the most relevant responses.

16. ChatGPT for Educators

Teaching is an art that requires creativity, dedication, and a constant drive to find new ways to inspire students. As AI continues to evolve, it can be a powerful ally for educators. ChatGPT, with its ability to comprehend and generate human-like text, can be a significant asset for educators.

This chapter provides practical examples as a guide on how educators can use it to enrich their teaching methods, create engaging learning materials, automate administrative tasks, and promote collaboration and discussion among students.

A. Few Ideas and Examples

1. Creating Lesson Plans

ChatGPT can assist educators in designing detailed lesson plans. By providing ChatGPT with a topic, grade level, and other relevant parameters, it can generate a step-by-step lesson plan, including learning objectives, teaching methods, and assessment strategies.

Example: If you are teaching a unit on ecosystems for a 5th-grade science class, you could prompt ChatGPT with something like, "Design a lesson plan for a 5th-grade science class about ecosystems.". ChatGPT could then create a lesson plan that includes a discussion of different types of ecosystems, hands-on activities, and assessments to measure students' understanding.

2. Developing Learning Materials

ChatGPT can assist in creating engaging learning materials, such as quizzes, worksheets, and study guides. It can also generate ideas for interactive learning activities.

Example: If you are teaching a unit on fractions and need to create a worksheet, you could ask ChatGPT, "Generate a worksheet on fractions for a 4th-grade math class.". ChatGPT might then create a worksheet that includes problems on adding, subtracting, multiplying, and dividing fractions.

3. Automating Administrative Tasks

ChatGPT can help with time-consuming administrative tasks, such as drafting emails or generating feedback for students. This allows educators to spend more time on instructional duties.

Example: If you need to send an email to parents about an upcoming parent-teacher conference, you could ask

ChatGPT, "Draft an email to parents about an upcoming parent-teacher conference.". ChatGPT could then create a professional and informative email, outlining the purpose of the conference, date and time, and any other relevant details.

4. Promoting Collaboration and Discussion

ChatGPT can be used to stimulate class discussions and foster a collaborative learning environment. It can provide topics for debates, generate open-ended questions for discussions, and provide ideas for group projects.

Example: If you are teaching a high school history class and want to start a discussion about the American Civil War, you could ask ChatGPT, "What are some open-ended discussion questions about the American Civil War for a high school history class?". ChatGPT might generate questions such as, "What were the long-term effects of the American Civil War?". or "How might American history have unfolded differently if the Civil War had not happened?".

5. Other Examples

- Grading assignments
- Ideas for classroom activities or projects
- Quizzes or tests based on curriculum content
- Language translation for multilingual students
- Summaries of educational research or articles

The possibilities are endless.

B. Applied Example: Creating Learning Materials

Here is a detailed simulation of how an educator might interact with ChatGPT to create a quiz on a specific topic.

Let's say you are teaching a unit on the solar system to your 6th-grade science class, and you need to create a quiz to assess your students' understanding. Here is how you might interact with ChatGPT:

```
User: I need to create a quiz for my 6th-grade science class on the solar system. The quiz should cover planets, their characteristics, and the concept of orbits. Can you help me create this?

ChatGPT: Absolutely! Here's a suggestion for the quiz:

1. Name the eight planets in our solar system, in order from the Sun.

2. Describe one unique characteristic of each planet.

3. What is an orbit and how does it apply to our solar system?

4. Which planet has the largest orbit around the Sun and why?

5. True or False: All planets in our solar system have moons.
```

User: These are great, but could we add a couple of more challenging questions for students who want to push themselves?

ChatGPT: Of course! Here are two more advanced questions:

6. Explain why different planets have different lengths of years.

7. Besides the eight planets, what are three other types of objects found in our solar system?

C. Exercises

Write prompts asking ChatGPT:
• To generate a lesson plan for a specific topic.
• To create a quiz or a worksheet for a specific subject.
• To recommend grading rubrics.
• To help write report card comments.
• For suggestions on classroom management strategies.
• For suggestions on using technology in the classroom.

D. Summary

In this chapter, we have explored how ChatGPT can be a powerful tool for educators. From creating lesson plans and engaging learning materials to automating administrative tasks and promoting collaboration and discussion, ChatGPT can enhance the educational experience. The key is understanding how to effectively communicate with ChatGPT through well-crafted prompts.

17. ChatGPT for Students

The life of a student is multifaceted and challenging, encompassing areas such as studying, assignment completion, research, time management, and preparation for the future. With the power of AI, specifically language models like ChatGPT, students can find significant assistance and enhance their learning experiences. This chapter will guide students with examples on how to utilize ChatGPT for their academic and personal growth.

It is imperative to remember the importance of academic integrity when using tools like ChatGPT. While it can assist in understanding concepts and generating ideas, students should ensure that any work submitted as their own truly reflects their understanding and effort. Relying too heavily on AI-generated content can undermine learning and violate academic honesty policies.

A. Few Ideas and Examples

1. Homework Assistance

ChatGPT can assist with homework by providing explanations, examples, and step-by-step guides for various subjects. It can also help with the revision of concepts learned in class.

Example: Suppose you are struggling with a topic in mathematics. You could ask ChatGPT, "Can you explain the concept of Pythagoras' theorem in a simple way?".

2. Essay Writing and Proofreading

ChatGPT can aid in structuring essays, generating ideas, providing feedback, and proofreading for grammatical errors and clarity.

Example: If you are writing an essay on climate change but cannot figure out how to start, you could ask ChatGPT, "What's a good introduction for an essay on the impacts of climate change?".

3. Study Planning and Time Management

ChatGPT can provide suggestions for creating study plans, managing time efficiently, and handling stress during exams.

Example: If you are preparing for final exams and feeling overwhelmed, you could ask ChatGPT, "How can I create an effective study plan for my final exams?".

4. Research Assistance

ChatGPT can assist in gathering information for research projects, suggesting sources, and providing summaries of complex materials.

Example: If you are working on a history project about the Renaissance period, you could ask ChatGPT, "What were the key events during the Renaissance period?".

5. Career Guidance

ChatGPT can provide information about various career paths, required qualifications, and potential colleges or universities to consider.

Example: If you are considering a career in software engineering, you could ask ChatGPT, "What are the necessary qualifications for a career in software engineering?".

6. Other Examples

- Thesis statements
- Practice for language learning or conversation skills
- Summarizing long articles or textbooks
- Preparation for quizzes or exams
- Coding help or debugging assistance for computer science students

The possibilities are endless.

B. Applied Example: Homework Assistance

Let's say you are studying for a biology test and you are struggling to understand the process of photosynthesis. Here is a simulation of how you might interact with ChatGPT:

User: I'm studying for a biology test and I'm struggling to understand photosynthesis. Can you explain this process in a simple way?

ChatGPT: Sure, here's a simplified explanation:

Photosynthesis is a process used by plants to convert light energy, usually from the Sun, into chemical energy that can be later released to fuel the plant's activities. This conversion is done in a series of steps inside the chloroplasts (a part of the plant cell):

1. **Light-dependent reactions**: Light energy is captured by chlorophyll in the plant's cells and is used to split water molecules into hydrogen and oxygen. The oxygen is released into the air as a waste product.

2. **Calvin cycle (light-independent reactions)**: The hydrogen is then used along with carbon dioxide from the air to create glucose (a type of sugar) through a series of reactions.

So, in short, photosynthesis takes in light energy, water, and carbon dioxide and produces glucose and oxygen.

```
This is a basic overview and the actual process has many more details, but hopefully, this helps you understand the main idea!
```

C. Exercises

Write prompts asking ChatGPT:
• To explain a concept you are struggling with.
• To proofread an essay introduction.
• For tips on managing time during exams.
• For information on a research topic.
• For information about a career you are interested in.

D. Summary

In this chapter, we have explored how ChatGPT can be a useful tool for students, assisting in areas such as homework, essay writing, study planning, research, and career guidance. By effectively utilizing AI, students can enhance their learning experiences and navigate their academic development more efficiently.

Remember, while ChatGPT aids learning, students must ensure that using it does not compromise their academic integrity or personal understanding.

18. ChatGPT for History Enthusiasts

History is a vast and fascinating field, filled with stories of people, events, and cultures from all over the world and throughout time. Whether you are a professional historian, a student, or simply someone with a keen interest in the past, ChatGPT can be a valuable tool for exploring historical topics, generating ideas for research, and even helping with the writing process.

This chapter will guide you with some relevant examples on how to leverage the power of ChatGPT to dig into historical topics, enhance your research efforts, and even assist in teaching history.

A. Few Ideas and Examples

1. Historical Research

ChatGPT can be a valuable tool for generating ideas for historical research. By providing it with a general topic or a set of parameters, it can generate a list of potential research questions or areas of focus.

Example: Suppose you are interested in the history of the Roman Empire. You might prompt ChatGPT with something like, "Generate a list of research questions about the Roman Empire.". ChatGPT could then provide a list of potential questions, such as "What were the key factors in the fall of the Roman Empire?" or "How did Roman law influence modern legal systems?".

2. Writing Assistance

ChatGPT can assist in creating compelling historical narratives, whether for academic papers, articles, or books. It can generate content for introductions, conclusions, and even entire sections of a paper.

Example: If you are writing a paper on the impact of the Industrial Revolution, you could ask ChatGPT, "Write an introduction for a paper on the impact of the Industrial Revolution.". ChatGPT might generate something like, "The Industrial Revolution, a period of rapid industrial growth that began in Great Britain in the 18th century and soon spread to other parts of the world, had profound effects on society, economy, and culture. This paper will explore the multifaceted impact of this transformative period, examining both its positive and negative consequences.".

3. Teaching History

ChatGPT can aid in creating lesson plans, study guides, and even interactive activities for teaching history. It can provide outlines, suggest key points to include, and even generate sections of the lesson.

Example: If you are a history teacher preparing a lesson on World War II, you might ask ChatGPT, "What are the key points to include in a lesson on World War II?". ChatGPT could provide a list of points to consider, such as the causes of the war, major events and battles, the role of different countries, and the war's aftermath.

4. Historical Trivia and Quizzes

ChatGPT can be used to generate historical trivia questions or quizzes, which can be a fun and engaging way to learn about history. This can be particularly useful for educators looking to create interactive learning experiences, or for history enthusiasts who enjoy testing their knowledge.

Example: If you are hosting a trivia night with a history theme, you might ask ChatGPT, "Generate ten trivia questions about the Samurai period in Japan.". ChatGPT could then provide a list of questions, such as "When did the Samurai period in Japan begin?" or "Who was the Shogun during the height of the Samurai era?".

5. Other Examples

- Summaries of historical events or periods
- List of recommended books, documentaries or other resources on a specific historical topic
- Insights into the cultural, social, or political context of a certain era
- Fictional narratives based on historical events or figures
- Research of genealogy or family history

The possibilities are endless.

B. Applied Example: Historical Research

Here is a detailed simulation of how a user might interact with ChatGPT to generate ideas for historical research.

Let's say you are studying the history of the United States and you are interested in the Civil Rights Movement. You want to come up with a unique research question for your term paper. Here is how you might interact with ChatGPT:

```
User: I need to come up with a research question for my term paper on the Civil Rights Movement in the United States. I'm particularly interested in the role of women in the movement. Can you help me craft a unique and compelling research question?
```

ChatGPT: Absolutely! Here's a suggestion:

How did women's roles in the Civil Rights Movement influence the development of the feminist movement in the United States?

User: That's a great question! Can we also include the impact of these women on the Civil Rights Movement itself?

ChatGPT: Of course! Here's the updated research question:

How did women's roles in the Civil Rights Movement not only influence the development of the feminist movement in the United States, but also shape the trajectory and outcomes of the Civil Rights Movement itself?

This example demonstrates how you can interact with ChatGPT iteratively, refining the output until you get the desired result. It is important to provide as much relevant information as possible in your prompts and to be specific about what you are asking for.

C. Exercises

Write prompts asking ChatGPT:

- To generate a list of research questions for a specific historical period or event.

Write prompts asking ChatGPT:
• To create an introduction for a paper on a specific historical topic.
• For the key points to include in a lesson on a specific historical period or event.
• Play the role of a historic character.
• To create a summary of historical events in a particular year or era.

D. Summary

In this chapter, we have explored the various ways ChatGPT can assist history enthusiasts. From generating innovative research questions and crafting compelling historical narratives, to aiding in lesson planning and teaching strategies, ChatGPT can be a valuable tool in your historical exploration.

19. ChatGPT for Scientific Research

Scientific research is a rigorous process that involves the systematic investigation of phenomena to establish facts and reach new conclusions. It requires a great deal of critical thinking, problem-solving, and creativity. In this digital age, AI has become a valuable tool for researchers, providing assistance in various tasks and decision-making processes.

It is vital to remember that while AI can aid in streamlining research processes, maintaining research integrity and accuracy is paramount. Always verify AI-generated information and do not solely rely on it for key findings or conclusions.

This chapter will guide you with some relevant examples on how to leverage the power of ChatGPT to assist in literature reviews, hypothesis generation, data analysis, and even in drafting research papers.

A. Few Ideas and Examples

1. Literature Reviews

ChatGPT can be a valuable tool for conducting scientific literature reviews. By providing it with a research topic or a set of parameters, it can generate a list of potential sources or summarize the key points from a given text.

Example: Suppose you are conducting research on the effects of climate change on marine life. You might provide an article and prompt ChatGPT with something like, "Summarize the key points from this article on the effects of climate change on coral reefs.". ChatGPT could then provide a summary of the article, highlighting the key findings and conclusions.

2. Hypothesis Generation

ChatGPT can assist in generating hypotheses for your research. It can provide suggestions based on the information it was trained on, helping you to think of new angles or perspectives for your research.

Example: If you are conducting a study on the effects of diet on mental health, you could ask ChatGPT, "Generate a list of potential hypotheses for a study on the effects of diet on mental health.". ChatGPT might generate a list of hypotheses, such as "A diet high in processed foods increases the risk of depression" or "A diet rich in fruits and vegetables improves cognitive function.".

3. Data Analysis

While ChatGPT cannot analyze data directly, unless it is integrated to a database, it can assist in interpreting the results of your data analysis. It can help you understand statistical concepts, generate insights from your results, and even suggest potential limitations or future directions for your research.

Example: If you are analyzing the results of a survey on consumer behavior, you might share the survey results and ask ChatGPT, "What are some potential insights from this survey that found a positive correlation between income and preference for organic products?". ChatGPT could provide a list of potential insights, such as the possibility that higher income individuals are more likely to afford organic products, or that they might be more aware of the benefits of organic products.

4. Drafting Research Papers

ChatGPT can aid in drafting research papers. It can provide outlines, suggest key points to include, and even generate sections of the paper. However, it is important to note that the outputs of ChatGPT should always be thoroughly reviewed and edited to ensure accuracy and adherence to academic standards.

Example: If you are drafting a research paper on the effects of air pollution on lung health, you might ask ChatGPT, "What are the key points to include in a research paper on the effects of air pollution on lung health?". ChatGPT could provide a list of points to consider, such as the types of air pollutants, their sources, the mechanisms by which they affect lung health, the populations most at risk, and the measures to mitigate air pollution.

5. Other Examples

- Research proposal drafts
- Research findings summaries
- Peer review process assistance
- Ideas for future research directions
- Conversational interface for scientific databases

The possibilities are endless.

B. Applied Example: Literature Reviews

Here is a detailed simulation of how a user might interact with ChatGPT to conduct a literature review.

Let's say you are conducting research on the effects of meditation on mental health. You have a number of research papers and articles to review, and you need help in summarizing the key points. Here is how you might interact with ChatGPT:

```
User: I need to summarize a research paper
titled "The Impact of Meditation on Mental Health:
```

A Comprehensive Review". The paper discusses various types of meditation, their effects on different mental health conditions, and the potential mechanisms behind these effects. Can you help me draft a summary?

ChatGPT: Absolutely! Here's a suggestion:

This comprehensive review explores the impact of various forms of meditation on mental health. The paper categorizes meditation techniques into several types and investigates their effects on a range of mental health conditions, including anxiety, depression, and stress-related disorders. The review finds consistent evidence supporting the positive effects of meditation on mental health, although the magnitude of these effects varies depending on the type of meditation and the specific mental health condition.

The paper also delves into potential mechanisms behind these effects, suggesting that meditation may work by modulating physiological responses to stress and improving emotional regulation. However, the authors note that more research is needed to fully understand these mechanisms and to determine the most effective meditation techniques for different mental health conditions.

User: That's a great summary! Can we also mention that the paper calls for more standardized and rigorous research methods in future studies on meditation and mental health?

ChatGPT: Of course! Here's the updated summary:

This comprehensive review explores the impact of various forms of meditation on mental health. The paper categorizes meditation techniques into several types and investigates their effects on a range of mental health conditions, including anxiety, depression, and stress-related disorders. The review finds consistent evidence supporting the positive effects of meditation on mental health, although the magnitude of these effects varies depending on the type of meditation and the specific mental health condition.

The paper also delves into potential mechanisms behind these effects, suggesting that meditation may work by modulating physiological responses to stress and improving emotional regulation. Despite these promising findings, the authors call for more standardized and rigorous research methods in future studies on meditation and mental health, to ensure the reliability and validity of the results. They also emphasize the need for more research to fully understand the mechanisms behind the effects of meditation and to determine the most effective meditation techniques for different mental health conditions.

This example simulation demonstrates how you can interact with ChatGPT iteratively, refining the output until you get the desired result. It is important to provide as much relevant information as possible in your prompts and to be specific about what you are asking for.

C. Exercises

Write prompts asking ChatGPT:
• To summarize a research article of your choice.
• To generate a hypothesis for a research topic of your choice.
• For potential insights from a hypothetical data analysis result.
• For the key points to include in a research paper on a specific topic.
• Analyze and compare research results.

D. Summary

In this chapter, we have explored the various ways ChatGPT can assist scientific researchers. From conducting literature reviews and generating hypotheses, to interpreting data analysis results and drafting research papers, ChatGPT can be a valuable tool in scientific research.

However, while ChatGPT can aid in streamlining research, it is vital to maintain research integrity, verify AI-generated information, and not solely rely on it for key conclusions.

20. ChatGPT for Engineering

Engineering is a diverse field that calls for creativity, precision, and a solid understanding of scientific principles. ChatGPT, with its ability to generate comprehensive, nuanced text, can be a great ally for engineers across various disciplines.

It is important to remember that while ChatGPT can aid in providing insights or generating ideas, the critical assessment, accuracy, safety, and ethical considerations of engineering tasks must always be maintained by the human engineer.

A. Few Ideas and Examples

1. Concept Development

ChatGPT can aid in the initial stages of engineering design, helping to brainstorm new concepts or providing feedback on existing ideas.

Example: If you are working on developing a new type of drone, you could ask ChatGPT, "Generate a list of innovative features for a next-generation drone.".

2. Design and Calculations

ChatGPT can assist with outlining design considerations, and it can also be used to cross-verify simple engineering calculations.

Example: If you are designing a pedestrian bridge, you might ask ChatGPT, "What are the key factors to consider when designing a pedestrian bridge?".

3. Review of Technical Documents

ChatGPT can assist with the review of technical documents, offering a second set of "eyes" to help catch any potential errors or inconsistencies.

Example: You could feed a portion of a technical report into ChatGPT and ask, "Please identify any potential inconsistencies or errors in the following report excerpt.".

4. Problem-Solving

Engineering often involves addressing complex, multi-faceted problems. ChatGPT can provide a platform for brainstorming solutions.

Example: If you are troubleshooting an issue with a solar panel array, you could ask ChatGPT, "What are some potential causes for reduced efficiency in a solar panel array?".

5. Other Examples

- Software debugging
- Evaluating engineering options
- Material selection for a project
- Project management
- Test scenario planning

The possibilities are endless.

B. Applied Example: Problem-Solving

Let's dig deeper into how an engineer might use ChatGPT for problem-solving. Suppose you are an electrical engineer working on a circuit design that is not functioning as expected. Here is how you might interact with ChatGPT:

User: I'm having an issue with a circuit design. It's a basic op-amp circuit but I'm not getting the gain I expected. What could be going wrong?

ChatGPT: There could be several reasons why you're not getting the expected gain in your op-amp circuit. Here are a few possibilities:

1. **Incorrect Resistor Values**: Check the resistors in your feedback loop. The gain of an op-amp circuit is often set by the ratio of these

```
resistors. Make sure they have the correct values
and are not faulty.

   2. Op-Amp Limits: Consider the limitations of
your op-amp. It might not be able to handle the
gain you're trying to achieve, either due to its
gain-bandwidth product or slew rate.

   3. Power Supply Issues: Verify your power supply
voltages. Improper power supply voltage could
affect the performance of your op-amp.

   4. Component Quality: Check the quality of your
components. Poor-quality components could lead to
poor performance.

   Remember to follow proper safety precautions
while testing and troubleshooting your circuit.
```

C. Exercises

Create prompts asking ChatGPT:
• To brainstorm ideas for a new engineering project.
• To review a section of a technical document.
• For problem-solving strategies for a complex engineering issue.
• To generate a list of project management tips for an engineering project.
• For properties of a material.

D. Summary

ChatGPT can be a great companion in the engineering field, aiding in concept development, design considerations, technical document review, and problem-solving.

However, human judgement remains crucial in ensuring accuracy, safety, and ethical adherence in all engineering tasks.

21. ChatGPT for Doctors/Health Care

Medicine and health care are fields that require a vast amount of knowledge and constant learning. In this digital age, AI has become a valuable tool for doctors and other health care professionals, providing assistance in various tasks and decision-making processes. ChatGPT, with its ability to understand and generate human-like text, can be a game-changer for doctors and health care professionals.

However, it is necessary to bear in mind the importance of patient privacy, data security, and professional integrity when using AI tools like ChatGPT in a healthcare setting. Any use of ChatGPT should be in compliance with medical ethics and privacy laws.

This chapter will guide you with some relevant examples on how to leverage the power of AI to assist in medical research, patient education, professional development, and even in managing your practice.

Remember, while ChatGPT can be a valuable tool, it should not replace professional medical advice or decision-making. Always consult with appropriate medical professionals and use your professional judgment in medical matters. The information provided in this book is for educational purposes only.

A. Few Ideas and Examples

1. Medical Research

ChatGPT can be a valuable tool for medical research. By providing it with a research question or a set of parameters, it can generate a list of potential research ideas or suggest improvements to your research design.

Example: Suppose you are interested in researching the effects of a new drug on heart disease. You might prompt ChatGPT with something like, "Generate a list of research questions for studying the effects of Drug X on heart disease.". ChatGPT could then provide a list of potential research questions, such as the impact of the drug on various heart disease markers, its side effects, or its efficacy compared to existing treatments.

2. Patient Education

ChatGPT can assist in educating patients about their health conditions and treatments. It can explain complex medical concepts in simple, understandable language.

Example: If you are trying to explain the concept of blood pressure to a patient, you could ask ChatGPT, "Explain the concept of blood pressure in simple terms.". ChatGPT might provide a simple and clear explanation that you can use to educate your patient.

3. Professional Development

ChatGPT can aid in your professional development. It can provide summaries of recent medical research, suggest potential areas for further study, and even help you prepare for presentations or teaching sessions.

Example: If you are preparing a presentation on diabetes treatment options, you might ask ChatGPT, "Summarize all the diabetes treatment options.". ChatGPT could provide a summary of the treatment options, which you can use to inform your presentation.

4. Practice Management

ChatGPT can assist in managing your medical practice. It can generate reminders for patient follow-ups, help draft professional emails, and even suggest strategies for improving patient satisfaction.

Example: If you are trying to improve patient satisfaction in your practice, you might ask ChatGPT, "What are some strategies for improving patient satisfaction in a medical practice?". ChatGPT might suggest strategies such as improving communication with patients, reducing wait times, or providing more patient education resources.

5. Other Examples

- Medical reports drafts
- Health and wellness content for patient outreach
- Preliminary responses to patient queries
- Personalized fitness and diet plans for patients
- Medical case study creation

The possibilities are endless.

B. Applied Example: Patient Education

Here is a detailed simulation of how a user might interact with ChatGPT to educate a patient about a health condition.

Let's say you are a doctor and you need to explain the concept of cholesterol to a patient. Here is how you might interact with ChatGPT:

```
User: I need to explain the concept of cholesterol to a patient in simple terms. Can you help me craft a clear and simple explanation?

ChatGPT: Absolutely! Here's a suggestion:

Cholesterol is a type of fat that's found in your blood. Your body needs some cholesterol to function properly, as it's used to build cells
```

and make certain hormones. However, too much cholesterol in your blood can be a problem. It can stick to the walls of your arteries, forming a hard substance called plaque. Over time, plaque can narrow your arteries and make it harder for blood to flow through them. This can lead to heart disease. There are two main types of cholesterol: LDL, often called 'bad' cholesterol, because it contributes to plaque buildup, and HDL, often called 'good' cholesterol, because it helps remove LDL from your bloodstream.

User: That's great! Can we also mention the importance of diet and exercise in managing cholesterol levels?

ChatGPT: Of course! Here's the updated explanation:

Cholesterol is a type of fat that's found in your blood. Your body needs some cholesterol to function properly, as it's used to build cells and make certain hormones. However, too much cholesterol in your blood can be a problem. It can stick to the walls of your arteries, forming a hard substance called plaque. Over time, plaque can narrow your arteries and make it harder for blood to flow through them. This can lead to heart disease. There are two main types of cholesterol: LDL, often called 'bad' cholesterol, because it contributes to plaque buildup, and HDL, often called 'good' cholesterol, because it helps remove LDL from your bloodstream.

It's important to know that diet and exercise play a crucial role in managing your cholesterol levels. Eating a healthy diet low in saturated fats and getting regular exercise can help lower

```
your LDL cholesterol and raise your HDL cholesterol.
```

This example demonstrates how you can interact with ChatGPT iteratively, refining the output until you get the desired result. It is important to provide as much relevant information as possible in your prompts and to be specific about what you are asking for.

C. Exercises

Write prompts asking ChatGPT to:
• Generate a list of research questions for a specific medical topic of your choice.
• Create a summary of recent research findings in a specific medical field.
• Provide strategies for improving patient satisfaction in a medical practice.
• Help you understand medical insurance from the viewpoints of Doctors, Patients and Insurers.
• Help you navigate hiring contractors in your practice.
• Explain strategies to manage moral injuries.

D. Summary

In this chapter, we have explored the various ways ChatGPT can assist doctors. From assisting in medical research and patient education, to aiding in professional development and practice management, ChatGPT can be a valuable tool in your medical practice.

However, it is critical to always respect patient privacy, maintain data security, adhere to professional integrity, and consult with appropriate medical professionals. Remember, ChatGPT should not replace professional medical decision-making.

22. ChatGPT for Lawyers

The legal profession is a field where precision, accuracy, and a deep understanding of complex laws are paramount. In this digital age, AI has become a valuable tool for lawyers, providing assistance in various tasks and decision-making processes.

This chapter will guide you with some relevant examples on how to leverage the power of ChatGPT to assist with legal research, drafting legal documents, preparing for court cases, and fostering effective client communication.

Please note that while ChatGPT can be a valuable tool, it is not a substitute for professional legal advice. Always consult with a qualified legal professional and verify the information provided by ChatGPT. The information provided in this book is for educational purposes only.

A. Few Ideas and Examples

1. Legal Research

ChatGPT can be a valuable tool for conducting legal research. By providing it with a specific legal question or a set of parameters, it can generate a list of potential legal sources precedents or case law. It can also help in summarizing and understanding complex legal texts.

Example: Suppose you are researching the legal implications of data privacy in the tech industry. You might prompt ChatGPT with something like, "Summarize the key points of the General Data Protection Regulation (GDPR) in the context of tech companies.". ChatGPT could then provide a summary of the GDPR, focusing on the aspects most relevant to tech companies.

2. Drafting Legal Documents

ChatGPT can assist in drafting legal documents such as contracts, agreements, and legal briefs. It can provide outlines, suggest key points to include, and even generate sections of the document.

Example:

If you are drafting a non-disclosure agreement (NDA), you might ask ChatGPT, "What are the key points to include in a non-disclosure agreement?". ChatGPT could provide a list of points to consider, such as the definition of confidential information, obligations of the receiving party, exclusions from confidential information, term of the agreement, and consequences of breach.

3. Preparing for Court Cases

ChatGPT can aid in preparing for court cases by helping to generate potential questions, summarize case law, and strategize arguments.

Example:

If you are preparing for a civil litigation case, you could ask ChatGPT, "What are some potential questions that the opposing counsel might ask my client?". ChatGPT might generate a list of potential questions based on the details of the case.

4. Client Communication

ChatGPT can help draft professional and clear communication with clients, such as emails, letters, and updates on their case.

Example:

If you need to update a client on the status of their case, you could ask ChatGPT, "Draft a professional email updating a client on the progress of their civil litigation case.". ChatGPT might generate a professional and clear email that provides the client with an update on their case.

5. Other Examples

- Complex legal cases summaries
- Training materials for law students and staff
- Simple explanations of complex legal terms
- Creation of legal articles or blogs
- Role playing based on a jury or judge scenario

The possibilities are endless.

B. Applied Example: Drafting Legal Documents

Here is a detailed simulation of how a user might interact with ChatGPT to draft a section of a legal document. Let's say you are drafting a contract and need assistance with the "Termination" clause. Here is how you might interact with ChatGPT:

```
User: I'm drafting a contract and need to write a termination clause. The contract is for a one-year consulting service, and either party should be able to terminate the contract with 30 days' notice. Can you help me draft this clause?

ChatGPT: Absolutely! Here's a suggestion:

Termination: Either party may terminate this Agreement by providing the other party with a written notice of termination at least thirty (30) days prior to the intended date of termination.
```

```
Upon termination, all obligations, duties, and responsibilities under this Agreement will cease, except for those obligations that by their nature are intended to survive termination (such as payment obligations). Termination of this Agreement will not affect any rights or obligations of the parties accrued prior to the effective date of termination.
```

User: That's great! Can we also mention that any breach of the contract terms would be grounds for immediate termination?

ChatGPT: Of course! Here's the updated clause:

Termination: Either party may terminate this Agreement by providing the other party with a written notice of termination at least thirty (30) days prior to the intended date of termination. Notwithstanding the foregoing, in the event of a material breach of this Agreement by either party, the non-breaching party may terminate this Agreement immediately upon written notice to the breaching party. Upon termination, all obligations, duties, and responsibilities under this Agreement will cease, except for those obligations that by their nature are intended to survive termination (such as payment obligations). Termination of this Agreement will not affect any rights or obligations of the parties accrued prior to the effective date of termination.

This example demonstrates how you can interact with ChatGPT iteratively, refining the output until you get the desired result. It is important to provide as much relevant information as possible in your prompts and to be specific about what you are asking for.

C. Exercises

Create prompts asking ChatGPT:
• To summarize a specific law or regulation.
• To draft a section of a legal document.
• For potential questions that might be asked in a specific type of court case.
• To draft a professional email to a client updating them on their case.
• To play the role of the opposite side of a legal argument.

D. Summary

In this chapter, we have explored the various ways ChatGPT can assist lawyers. From conducting legal research and drafting legal documents, to preparing for court cases and communicating with clients, ChatGPT can be a valuable tool in your legal practice. Always verify the information provided by ChatGPT and consult with a qualified legal professional as necessary.

23. ChatGPT for Real Estate Agents

The real estate industry is a dynamic field where effective communication, market knowledge, and negotiation skills are key. In this digital age, AI has become a valuable tool for real estate agents, providing assistance in various tasks and decision-making processes.

This chapter will guide you with some relevant examples on how to leverage the power of ChatGPT to assist with property research, drafting property descriptions, preparing for client meetings, and fostering effective client communication. Please note that while ChatGPT can be a valuable tool, it is not a substitute for professional real estate advice. Always consult with a qualified real estate professional and verify the information provided by ChatGPT.

A. Few Ideas and Examples

1. Property Research

ChatGPT can be a valuable tool for conducting property research. By providing it with a specific question or a set of parameters, it can generate a list of potential properties or market trends. It can also help in summarizing and understanding complex real estate data.

Example: Suppose you are researching the real estate market trends in a specific neighborhood. You might prompt ChatGPT with something like, "Summarize the key real estate market trends in the Downtown district of City X.". ChatGPT could then provide a summary of the market trends, focusing on the aspects most relevant to your query.

2. Drafting Property Descriptions

ChatGPT can assist in drafting property descriptions that are compelling and engaging. It can provide outlines, suggest key points to include, and even generate sections of the description.

Example: If you are drafting a property description for a residential property, you might ask ChatGPT, "What are the key points to include in a property description for a 3-bedroom residential property?". ChatGPT could provide a list of points to consider, such as the location, size, unique features, nearby amenities, and price.

3. Preparing for Client Meetings

ChatGPT can aid in preparing for client meetings by helping to generate potential questions, summarize client preferences, and strategize negotiation tactics.

Example: If you are preparing for a client meeting, you could ask ChatGPT, "What are some potential questions that I should ask my client during our first meeting?". ChatGPT might generate a list of potential questions based on the details of the client's property needs and preferences.

4. Client Communication

ChatGPT can help draft professional and clear communication with clients, such as emails, letters, and updates on their property search or sale.

Example: If you need to update a client on the status of their property search, you could ask ChatGPT, "Draft a professional email updating a client on the progress of their property search.". ChatGPT might generate a professional and clear email that provides the client with an update on their property search.

5. Other Examples

- Real estate market reports
- Blog posts or articles on real estate topics
- Ideas for marketing campaigns
- Scripts for virtual property tours

- Neighborhood analysis

The possibilities are endless.

B. Applied Example: Drafting Property Descriptions

Here is a detailed simulation of how a user might interact with ChatGPT to draft a property description. Let's say you are listing a residential property and need assistance with the property description. Here is how you might interact with ChatGPT:

```
User: I'm listing a residential property and need to write a compelling property description. The property is a 3-bedroom, 2-bathroom house with a large backyard, modern kitchen, and is located in a quiet neighborhood close to good schools. Can you help me draft this description?

ChatGPT: Absolutely! Here's a suggestion:

Welcome to your dream home! This charming 3-bedroom, 2-bathroom house is nestled in a serene neighborhood, offering peace and quiet while being conveniently close to top-rated schools. The spacious backyard provides ample space for outdoor activities and gardening. Inside, you'll find a modern kitchen equipped with state-of-the-art appliances, perfect for the home chef. The open floor plan allows for easy flow between the kitchen, dining area, and living room, making it an ideal space for entertaining. Each bedroom offers plenty of space and comfort, and the master suite features a private bathroom. This home
```

```
offers the perfect blend of comfort,
functionality, and location. Don't miss out on
this gem!


User: That's great! Can we also mention that
the house has a finished basement and a two-car
garage?

ChatGPT: Of course! Here's the updated
description:

Welcome to your dream home! This charming 3-
bedroom, 2-bathroom house is nestled in a serene
neighborhood, offering peace and quiet while being
conveniently close to top-rated schools. Inside,
you'll find a modern kitchen equipped with state-
of-the-art appliances, perfect for the home chef.
The open floor plan allows for easy flow between
the kitchen, dining area, and living room, making
it an ideal space for entertaining. The house also
boasts a finished basement, providing extra space
for a home office, gym, or playroom.

A spacious two-car garage and a large backyard
further enhance the appeal of this property. Each
bedroom offers plenty of space and comfort, and
the master suite features a private bathroom. This
home offers the perfect blend of comfort,
functionality, and location. Don't miss out on
this gem!
```

This example demonstrates how you can interact with ChatGPT iteratively, refining the output until you get the desired result. It is important to provide as much relevant information as possible in your prompts and to be specific about what you are asking for.

C. Exercises

Write prompts asking ChatGPT:
• To summarize a specific real estate market trend.
• To draft a property description.
• For potential questions that might be asked during a client meeting.
• To draft a professional email to a client updating them on their property search.
• To create comparison of properties for a client.

D. Summary

In this chapter, we have explored the various ways ChatGPT can assist real estate agents. From conducting property research and drafting property descriptions, to preparing for client meetings and communicating with clients, ChatGPT can be a valuable tool in your real estate practice. Always verify the information provided by ChatGPT and consult with a qualified real estate professional as necessary.

24. ChatGPT for Musicians

Music is a universal language that transcends cultural and linguistic boundaries. It is a form of expression that allows us to communicate emotions and ideas in a unique way. In this digital age, AI has become a valuable tool for musicians, providing assistance in various tasks and creative processes.

While using tools like ChatGPT, musicians must always respect copyright laws, and maintain the authenticity and integrity of their own creative voice. The use of ChatGPT should enhance and inspire musical creativity, not replace it.

This chapter will guide you with some relevant examples on how to leverage the power of ChatGPT to assist in songwriting, music theory, music production, and even in promoting your music.

A. Few Ideas and Examples

1. Songwriting

ChatGPT can be a valuable tool for songwriting. By providing it with a theme, a set of lyrics, or a melody, it can generate a song or suggest improvements to your lyrics.

Example: Suppose you are writing a song about the feeling of falling in love. You might prompt ChatGPT with something like, "Write a verse and a chorus for a pop song about falling in love.". ChatGPT could then provide a verse and a chorus that captures the joy and excitement of falling in love.

2. Music Theory

ChatGPT can assist in understanding music theory. It can explain complex concepts, provide examples, and even help you apply music theory to your compositions.

Example: If you are struggling to understand the concept of harmonic progression, you could ask ChatGPT, "Explain the concept of harmonic progression in music theory.". ChatGPT might provide a simple and clear explanation, along with examples to help you understand the concept.

3. Music Production

While ChatGPT cannot produce music directly, it can assist in the music production process. It can provide tips on mixing and mastering, suggest potential effects or adjustments, and even help you troubleshoot issues in your music production software.

Example: If you are having trouble achieving a balanced mix in your song, you might ask ChatGPT, "What are some tips for achieving a balanced mix in a pop song?". ChatGPT could provide a list of tips, such as adjusting the levels of different tracks, using techniques to avoid frequency clashes, and applying compression to control dynamics.

4. Music Promotion

ChatGPT can aid in promoting your music. It can generate engaging social media posts, write press releases, and even suggest strategies for reaching a wider audience.

Example: If you are releasing a new album and want to create a social media post to announce the release, you might ask ChatGPT, "Write a catchy social media post to announce the release of my new album.". ChatGPT might generate something like, "The wait is finally over! My new album is out now and I can't wait for you to hear it. Each song is a piece of my heart and soul, and I hope they resonate with you as much as they do with me. #NewMusic #AlbumRelease".

5. Other Examples

- Music video concepts
- Suggestions for album or song titles
- Ideas for concert setlists

- Prompts for improvisation exercises
- Music theory tutorials or articles

The possibilities are endless.

B. Applied Example: Songwriting

Here is a detailed simulation of how a user might interact with ChatGPT to write a song.

Let's say you are writing a folk song about a journey. You have a basic idea for the melody and the theme, but you are struggling with the lyrics. Here is how you might interact with ChatGPT:

```
User: I'm writing a folk song about a journey. The melody has a nostalgic feel to it. Can you help me write the first verse and chorus?

ChatGPT: Absolutely! Here's a suggestion:

Verse 1:

On a dusty road, under the open sky,

I set off alone, with a dream in my eye.

The wind whispers tales, as I walk on by,

Of distant lands, where the mountains touch the sky.



Chorus:
```

```
Follow the road, let your heart be your guide,

Through the valleys and hills, with the stars as your light.

Every step is a story, every mile a song,

On this journey we're on, where we all belong.


User: That's great! Can we also mention the feeling of longing for home in the chorus?

ChatGPT: Of course! Here's the updated chorus:

Follow the road, let your heart be your guide,

Through the valleys and hills, with the stars as your light.

Every step is a story, every mile a song,

On this journey we're on, where we all belong.

And though we wander far, our hearts yearn for home,

In every melody, in every poem.
```

This example demonstrates how you can interact with ChatGPT iteratively, refining the output until you get the desired result. It is important to provide as much relevant information as possible in your prompts and to be specific about what you are asking for.

C. Exercises

Write prompts asking ChatGPT:
• To generate a verse for a song of your choice.
• To explain a concept in music theory.
• For tips on a specific aspect of music production.
• To create a social media post promoting your music.
• To suggestion options for revising a composition.

D. Summary

In this chapter, we have explored the various ways ChatGPT can assist musicians. From assisting in songwriting and understanding music theory, to aiding in music production and promotion, ChatGPT can be a valuable tool for musicians.

However, musicians should remember to respect copyright laws, maintain originality, and use AI as a tool for inspiration, not as a replacement for personal creativity.

25. ChatGPT for Artists

Artists thrive on creativity, inspiration, and technique. ChatGPT can assist artists by providing innovative ideas, art history insights, constructive criticism, and even assistance with teaching art.

While ChatGPT can provide inspiration and information, artists should respect copyright laws, maintain their originality, and use AI as a creative supplement rather than a replacement for personal expression and imagination.

This chapter will guide you with examples on how ChatGPT can be a valuable tool for artists.

A. Few Ideas and Examples

1. Idea Generation and Inspiration

ChatGPT can generate unique art project ideas and provide inspiration when you are feeling stuck.

Example: If you are facing artist's block, you might ask ChatGPT, "Give me an innovative idea for a mixed media art project.".

2. Art History and Techniques

ChatGPT can provide information on art history, famous artists, different art techniques, and styles.

Example: If you are interested in exploring Impressionism, you could ask ChatGPT, "Explain the characteristics of Impressionism and notable artists in this movement.".

3. Art Criticism and Improvement

ChatGPT can provide constructive feedback on your art pieces and suggest ways to improve.

Example: You could describe a painting you are working on to ChatGPT and ask, "How can I improve the composition of my painting?".

4. Teaching Art

ChatGPT can assist art teachers with lesson plans, project ideas, and explanations of complex art concepts.

Example: If you are an art teacher looking for a new project for your students, you might ask ChatGPT, "Suggest a fun and educational art project for fifth graders.".

5. Other Examples

- Sketch prompts
- Color palette suggestions
- Art marketing and social media promotion
- Artwork title suggestions
- Art Material Selection

The possibilities are endless.

B. Applied Example: Art Criticism and Improvement

Let's review a detailed interaction with ChatGPT where it assists in critiquing and improving an artwork. Suppose you are working on a landscape painting but feel something is off. Here is how you might interact with ChatGPT:

> **User**: I'm working on a landscape painting. It's a sunset scene with a large tree in the foreground, a lake in the mid-ground, and mountains in the background. I've used warm colors for the sunset and cool colors for the rest of the scene. But somehow, the painting doesn't seem balanced. What could I do to improve it?
>
> **ChatGPT**: It sounds like you have a good start. A few suggestions could be:
>
> 1. **Consider the rule of thirds**: Instead of placing the tree directly in the center, try shifting it to either side of the canvas.

```
2. **Add some warm colors elsewhere**: To balance the warm sunset, add subtle warm reflections on the lake and mountains.

3. **Play with light and shadow**: Make sure the tree's shadow is consistent with the light source (the sunset). The contrast of light and shadow can also add depth to your painting.
```

C. Exercises

Write prompts asking ChatGPT:
• For an innovative art project idea.
• For information on an art movement or technique.
• For critique on an artwork description.
• For an art lesson plan idea.
• To provide analysis of a color palette in terms of emotional impact.

D. Summary

ChatGPT can aid artists with inspiration, advice, criticism, and teaching. While providing clear prompts is key, maintaining originality, respecting copyright, and using AI to supplement, not replace, personal creativity is essential.

26. ChatGPT for Creative Writing

Creative writing is a field that thrives on imagination, originality, and the ability to captivate readers with words. In this digital age, AI has become a valuable tool for creative writers, providing assistance in various tasks and decision-making processes. ChatGPT, with its ability to understand and generate human-like text, can provide a creative boost for writers.

This chapter will guide you with some relevant examples on how to leverage the power of ChatGPT to assist with story generation, character development, plot outlining, and fostering effective collaboration. While ChatGPT can be a valuable tool, it is not a substitute for professional writing practices. Always verify the content provided by ChatGPT and follow best practices in creative writing.

A. Few Ideas and Examples

1. Story Generation

ChatGPT can be a valuable tool for generating story ideas. By providing it with a specific genre or a set of parameters, it can generate a story idea or a plot.

Example: Suppose you are writing a science fiction story and need some inspiration. You might prompt ChatGPT with something like, "Generate a science fiction story idea involving time travel.". ChatGPT could then provide a unique and intriguing story idea involving time travel.

2. Character Development

ChatGPT can assist in developing characters by suggesting character traits, backstories, and potential character arcs. It can provide insights into character development and suggest changes to make the characters more compelling.

Example: If you are developing a character for your novel and need some inspiration, you might ask ChatGPT, "Generate a character profile for a protagonist in a fantasy novel.". ChatGPT could provide a detailed character profile, including the character's background, personality traits, strengths, weaknesses, and potential character arc.

3. Plot Outlining

ChatGPT can aid in outlining plots by providing a structured outline of the story, demonstrating how to arrange the events, and generating practice exercises.

Example: If you are outlining a mystery novel and want to understand how to structure the plot, you could ask ChatGPT, "Outline a plot for a mystery novel involving a stolen artifact.". ChatGPT might provide a detailed plot outline, including the introduction, rising action, climax, falling action, and resolution.

4. Collaboration

ChatGPT can help foster effective collaboration by generating clear and concise feedback, assisting in brainstorming sessions, and suggesting best practices for collaboration in creative writing.

Example: If you are working on a collaborative writing project and need to provide feedback, you could ask ChatGPT, "What are some best practices for providing constructive feedback in a creative writing project?". ChatGPT might provide a list of best practices for providing constructive feedback.

5. Other Examples

- Unique and interesting plot twists
- Dialogue for characters

27. ChatGPT for Entertainment

Entertainment is a field that thrives on creativity, originality, and the ability to captivate audiences. In this digital age, AI has become a valuable tool for entertainment, providing assistance in various tasks and decision-making processes. ChatGPT, with its ability to understand and generate human-like text, can be transformational for those in the entertainment industry.

This chapter will guide you with some relevant examples on how to leverage the power of ChatGPT to assist with scriptwriting, joke generation, game development, and fostering effective collaboration. Please note that while ChatGPT can be a valuable tool, it is not a substitute for professional practices in the entertainment industry. Always verify the content provided by ChatGPT and follow best practices in your field.

- World-building in fantasy or sci-fi stories
- "Second opinion" on story arcs or character development
- Ideas for titles of books, chapters, or short stories

The possibilities are endless.

B. Applied Example: Story Generation

Here is a detailed simulation of how a user might interact with ChatGPT to generate a story idea. Let's say you are working on a fantasy novel and need some inspiration for a new plot. Here is how you might interact with ChatGPT:

> **User**: I'm writing a fantasy novel and need some inspiration for a new plot. The story should involve a magical artifact and a journey to a forgotten kingdom. Can you help me generate a plot?
>
> **ChatGPT**: Absolutely! Here's a suggestion:
>
> In a world where magic is the norm, a young apprentice named Elysia discovers a forgotten artifact that holds the power to control time. The artifact, however, is incomplete, and the only way to unlock its full potential is to journey to the forgotten kingdom of Eldoria, a land lost in time and shrouded in mystery. Eldoria was once a thriving kingdom known for its advanced magic and technology, but it disappeared overnight, leaving behind only legends and myths.

Elysia decides to embark on a journey to Eldoria, guided by the artifact and the cryptic clues left behind in ancient texts. Along the way, she encounters various challenges, from magical creatures to complex riddles, testing her magic and her wits. As she delves deeper into the mystery of Eldoria, she uncovers secrets about the kingdom's downfall and the true nature of her artifact. The journey transforms Elysia, teaching her the values of courage, friendship, and the true meaning of power.

In the climax, Elysia must confront a powerful adversary who seeks to claim the artifact and use its power for destructive purposes. The confrontation leads to a thrilling battle of magic and wits, with the fate of magic itself hanging in the balance.

User: That's a great start! Can we also include a loyal companion for Elysia on her journey?

ChatGPT: Of course! Here's the updated plot:

Elysia doesn't embark on her journey alone. She is accompanied by her loyal companion, a shape-shifting creature named Rael. Rael has been Elysia's friend since childhood and has a mysterious past of his own. Together, they navigate the challenges and uncover the secrets of Eldoria. Rael's shape-shifting abilities and quick thinking often help them out of tricky situations, and his unwavering loyalty to Elysia adds an emotional depth to their journey.

This example demonstrates how you can interact with ChatGPT iteratively, refining the output until you get the desired result. It is important to provide as much relevant information as possible in your prompts and to be specific about what you are asking for.

C. Exercises

Write prompts asking ChatGPT:
• To generate a story idea for a specific genre.
• To create a character profile for a character in your story.
• To outline a plot for a story involving a specific event or theme.
• For best practices in collaborative creative writing.
• To compare several endings for your short story.

D. Summary

In this chapter, we have explored the various ways ChatGPT can assist creative writers. From generating story ideas and assisting with character development, to aiding in plot outlining and fostering effective collaboration, ChatGPT can be a valuable tool in your creative writing practice. Always verify the content provided by ChatGPT and follow best practices in creative writing.

- World-building in fantasy or sci-fi stories
- "Second opinion" on story arcs or character development
- Ideas for titles of books, chapters, or short stories

The possibilities are endless.

B. Applied Example: Story Generation

Here is a detailed simulation of how a user might interact with ChatGPT to generate a story idea. Let's say you are working on a fantasy novel and need some inspiration for a new plot. Here is how you might interact with ChatGPT:

User: I'm writing a fantasy novel and need some inspiration for a new plot. The story should involve a magical artifact and a journey to a forgotten kingdom. Can you help me generate a plot?

ChatGPT: Absolutely! Here's a suggestion:

In a world where magic is the norm, a young apprentice named Elysia discovers a forgotten artifact that holds the power to control time. The artifact, however, is incomplete, and the only way to unlock its full potential is to journey to the forgotten kingdom of Eldoria, a land lost in time and shrouded in mystery. Eldoria was once a thriving kingdom known for its advanced magic and technology, but it disappeared overnight, leaving behind only legends and myths.

Elysia decides to embark on a journey to Eldoria, guided by the artifact and the cryptic clues left behind in ancient texts. Along the way, she encounters various challenges, from magical creatures to complex riddles, testing her magic and her wits. As she delves deeper into the mystery of Eldoria, she uncovers secrets about the kingdom's downfall and the true nature of her artifact. The journey transforms Elysia, teaching her the values of courage, friendship, and the true meaning of power.

In the climax, Elysia must confront a powerful adversary who seeks to claim the artifact and use its power for destructive purposes. The confrontation leads to a thrilling battle of magic and wits, with the fate of magic itself hanging in the balance.

User: That's a great start! Can we also include a loyal companion for Elysia on her journey?

ChatGPT: Of course! Here's the updated plot:

Elysia doesn't embark on her journey alone. She is accompanied by her loyal companion, a shape-shifting creature named Rael. Rael has been Elysia's friend since childhood and has a mysterious past of his own. Together, they navigate the challenges and uncover the secrets of Eldoria. Rael's shape-shifting abilities and quick thinking often help them out of tricky situations, and his unwavering loyalty to Elysia adds an emotional depth to their journey.

This example demonstrates how you can interact with ChatGPT iteratively, refining the output until you get the desired result. It is important to provide as much relevant information as possible in your prompts and to be specific about what you are asking for.

C. Exercises

Write prompts asking ChatGPT:
• To generate a story idea for a specific genre.
• To create a character profile for a character in your story.
• To outline a plot for a story involving a specific event or theme.
• For best practices in collaborative creative writing.
• To compare several endings for your short story.

D. Summary

In this chapter, we have explored the various ways ChatGPT can assist creative writers. From generating story ideas and assisting with character development, to aiding in plot outlining and fostering effective collaboration, ChatGPT can be a valuable tool in your creative writing practice. Always verify the content provided by ChatGPT and follow best practices in creative writing.

27. ChatGPT for Entertainment

Entertainment is a field that thrives on creativity, originality, and the ability to captivate audiences. In this digital age, AI has become a valuable tool for entertainment, providing assistance in various tasks and decision-making processes. ChatGPT, with its ability to understand and generate human-like text, can be transformational for those in the entertainment industry.

This chapter will guide you with some relevant examples on how to leverage the power of ChatGPT to assist with scriptwriting, joke generation, game development, and fostering effective collaboration. Please note that while ChatGPT can be a valuable tool, it is not a substitute for professional practices in the entertainment industry. Always verify the content provided by ChatGPT and follow best practices in your field.

A. Few Ideas and Examples

1. Scriptwriting

ChatGPT can be a valuable tool for generating script ideas. By providing it with a specific genre or a set of parameters, it can generate a script or a plot.

Example: Suppose you are writing a comedy script and need some inspiration. You might prompt ChatGPT with something like, "Generate a comedy script involving a mistaken identity.". ChatGPT could then provide a unique and intriguing script involving mistaken identity.

2. Joke Generation

ChatGPT can assist in generating jokes by suggesting punchlines, setups, and joke structures. It can provide insights into joke writing and suggest changes to make the jokes more compelling.

Example: If you are writing a stand-up comedy set and need some new material, you might ask ChatGPT, "Generate a series of jokes about being a parent.". ChatGPT could provide a series of parent-themed jokes that you could incorporate into your set.

3. Game Development

ChatGPT can aid in developing game plots by providing a structured outline of the story, demonstrating how to arrange the events, and generating practice exercises.

Example: If you are developing a video game and want to understand how to structure the plot, you could ask ChatGPT, "Outline a plot for a fantasy video game involving a quest to find a magical artifact.". ChatGPT might provide a detailed plot outline, including the introduction, rising action, climax, falling action, and resolution.

4. Interactive Storytelling

ChatGPT can be used to create interactive storytelling experiences. It can generate different paths for a story based on user choices, creating a unique and engaging narrative each time.

Example: Suppose you are creating an interactive story for a mobile app. You could use ChatGPT to generate different story paths based on user choices. For instance, you might prompt ChatGPT with, "Generate a storyline for an interactive mystery story where the user chooses whether to follow clue A or clue B.". ChatGPT could then generate two different story paths based on the user's choice, creating a dynamic and engaging storytelling experience.

5. Other Examples

- Dialogues, character backstories, or plotlines for video games
- Ideas for role-playing games
- Creative themes for events, parties, or festivals
- Narratives or stories around magic tricks
- Video content scripts

The possibilities are endless.

B. Applied Example: Scriptwriting

Here is a detailed simulation of how a user might interact with ChatGPT to generate a script idea. Let's say you are working on a comedy script and need some inspiration for a new plot. Here is how you might interact with ChatGPT:

```
User: I'm writing a comedy script and need some inspiration for a new plot. The story should involve a case of mistaken identity and a series of hilarious misunderstandings. Can you help me generate a plot?

ChatGPT: Absolutely! Here's a suggestion:

In the bustling city of New York, a humble pizza delivery guy, Tony, is mistaken for a famous Italian fashion designer due to a mix-up at a fancy hotel. The real designer is in town for the biggest fashion event of the year, but he's nowhere to be found. Tony decides to go along with the misunderstanding, leading to a series of
```

hilarious situations as he tries to navigate the world of high fashion with his street-smart wit and pizza-making skills.

Meanwhile, the real designer ends up delivering pizzas across the city, experiencing a slice of life he's never known before. As the fashion event approaches, Tony must pull off the biggest bluff of his life, while the real designer discovers a newfound appreciation for the simple joys of life. The climax involves a fashion show featuring pizza-inspired outfits and a surprise appearance by the real designer, leading to a heartwarming and hilarious resolution.

User: That's a great start! Can we also include a love interest for Tony in the plot?

ChatGPT: Of course! Here's the updated plot:

In the bustling city of New York, a humble pizza delivery guy, Tony, is mistaken for a famous Italian fashion designer due to a mix-up at a fancy hotel. The real designer is in town for the biggest fashion event of the year, but he's nowhere to be found. Tony decides to go along with the misunderstanding, leading to a series of hilarious situations as he tries to navigate the world of high fashion with his street-smart wit and pizza-making skills.

Along the way, Tony meets Bella, a hardworking event organizer who's under the impression that he's the famous designer. Despite the mix-up, they form a genuine connection, adding a romantic twist to the comedy. Meanwhile, the real designer ends

```
up delivering pizzas across the city, experiencing
a slice of life he's never known before.

   As the fashion event approaches, Tony must pull
off the biggest bluff of his life, while also
winning Bella's heart. The climax involves a
fashion show featuring pizza-inspired outfits, a
surprise appearance by the real designer, and a
heartfelt confession from Tony, leading to a
heartwarming and hilarious resolution.
```

This example demonstrates how you can interact with ChatGPT iteratively, refining the output until you get the desired result. It is important to provide as much relevant information as possible in your prompts and to be specific about what you are asking for.

C. Exercises

Write prompts asking ChatGPT:
• To generate a script idea for a specific genre.
• To create a joke about a specific topic.
• To outline a plot for a video game involving a specific theme.
• To refine a stand-up comedy routine.
• For ideas on creating shows for a particular event.

D. Summary

In this chapter, we have explored the various ways ChatGPT can assist those in the entertainment industry. From generating script ideas and assisting with joke writing, to aiding in game development and fostering effective collaboration, ChatGPT can be a valuable tool in your entertainment practice. Always verify the content provided by ChatGPT and follow best practices in your field.

28. ChatGPT for Exercise and Fitness

Exercise and fitness are essential components of a healthy lifestyle. In this digital age, AI has become a valuable tool for fitness enthusiasts and professionals alike, providing assistance in various tasks and decision-making processes. ChatGPT, with its ability to understand and generate human-like text, can transform the fitness industry.

This chapter will guide you with some relevant examples on how to leverage the power of ChatGPT to assist with workout planning, diet advice, fitness goal setting, and fostering effective collaboration. While ChatGPT can be a valuable tool, it is not a substitute for professional advice in the fitness industry. Always verify the content provided by ChatGPT and follow best practices in your field.

A. Few Ideas and Examples

1. Workout Planning

ChatGPT can be a valuable tool for generating workout plans. By providing it with a specific goal or a set of parameters, it can generate a workout plan tailored to your needs.

Example: Suppose you are looking to build muscle and need a workout plan. You might prompt ChatGPT with something like, "Generate a 4-week workout plan for muscle building.". ChatGPT could then provide a detailed workout plan, including exercises, sets, reps, and rest periods.

2. Diet Advice

ChatGPT can assist in generating diet plans by suggesting meal ideas, portion sizes, and nutritional information. It can provide insights into healthy eating and suggest changes to make your diet more balanced.

Example: If you are trying to lose weight and need some diet advice, you might ask ChatGPT, "Generate a 7-day diet plan for weight loss.". ChatGPT could provide a detailed diet plan, including meal ideas and portion sizes.

3. Fitness Goal Setting

ChatGPT can aid in setting fitness goals by providing a structured outline of the goal, demonstrating how to track progress, and generating practice exercises.

Example: If you are looking to run a marathon and want to understand how to set a training goal, you could ask ChatGPT, "Outline a training plan for a marathon.". ChatGPT might provide a detailed training plan, including running distances, rest days, and cross-training days.

4. Yoga and Meditation Guidance

ChatGPT can be used to generate yoga sequences or meditation guides. By providing it with your level of expertise or specific focus areas, it can tailor a yoga sequence or meditation guide to your needs.

Example: Suppose you are a beginner in yoga and want to focus on flexibility. You might prompt ChatGPT with something like, "Generate a beginner-friendly yoga sequence for improving flexibility.". ChatGPT could then provide a sequence of yoga poses aimed at enhancing flexibility. Similarly, if you are looking for a guided meditation to reduce stress, you could ask ChatGPT, "Create a 10-minute guided meditation script for stress relief.". ChatGPT could then generate a calming and soothing meditation script.

5. Other Examples

- Yoga practice plan or benefits of different poses
- Meditation scripts or mindfulness exercises
- Tips on proper exercise techniques to prevent injuries
- Fitness challenges or goals for users to achieve
- Recovery Routines for cool down or recovery days

The possibilities are endless.

B. Applied Example: Workout Planning

Here is a detailed simulation of how a user might interact with ChatGPT to generate a workout plan. Let's say you are looking to build muscle and need a workout plan. Here is how you might interact with ChatGPT:

User: I'm looking to build muscle and need a 4-week workout plan. The plan should involve weightlifting exercises and should be suitable for a beginner. Can you help me generate a plan?

ChatGPT: Absolutely! Here's a suggestion:

Here's a simple 4-week workout plan for muscle building suitable for a beginner:

Week 1 & 2:

Day 1: Chest and Triceps - Bench Press, Incline Dumbbell Press, Tricep Dips, Skull Crushers

Day 2: Rest

Day 3: Back and Biceps - Deadlift, Bent Over Rows, Pull-ups, Barbell Curls

Day 4: Rest

Day 5: Legs and Shoulders - Squats, Lunges, Overhead Press, Lateral Raises

Day 6: Rest

Day 7: Rest

Week 3 & 4:

Day 1: Chest and Triceps - Incline Bench Press, Dumbbell Flyes, Tricep Pushdowns, Overhead Tricep Extension

Day 2: Rest

Day 3: Back and Biceps - Pull-ups, One-Arm Dumbbell Rows, Hammer Curls, Preacher Curls

Day 4: Rest

Day 5: Legs and Shoulders - Front Squats, Leg Press, Seated Dumbbell Press, Face Pulls

Day 6: Rest

Day 7: Rest

For each exercise, aim for 3 sets of 8-12 reps. Remember to start with light weights and focus on your form. Gradually increase the weights as you get stronger. Always warm up before starting your workout and cool down afterwards."

User: That's great! Can we also include some cardio in the plan?

ChatGPT: Of course! Here's the updated plan:

Here's a simple 4-week workout plan for muscle building and cardio suitable for a beginner:

Week 1 & 2:

Day 1: Chest and Triceps - Bench Press, Incline Dumbbell Press, Tricep Dips, Skull Crushers

Day 2: Cardio - 30 minutes of moderate-intensity cardio, such as brisk walking or cycling

Day 3: Back and Biceps - Deadlift, Bent Over Rows, Pull-ups, Barbell Curls

Day 4: Cardio - 30 minutes of moderate-intensity cardio, such as brisk walking or cycling

Day 5: Legs and Shoulders - Squats, Lunges, Overhead Press, Lateral Raises

Day 6: Rest

Day 7: Rest

Week 3 & 4:

```
Day 1: Chest and Triceps - Incline Bench Press, Dumbbell Flyes, Tricep Pushdowns, Overhead Tricep Extension

Day 2: Cardio - 30 minutes of moderate-intensity cardio, such as brisk walking or cycling

Day 3: Back and Biceps - Pull-ups, One-Arm Dumbbell Rows, Hammer Curls, Preacher Curls

Day 4: Cardio - 30 minutes of moderate-intensity cardio, such as brisk walking or cycling

Day 5: Legs and Shoulders - Front Squats, Leg Press, Seated Dumbbell Press, Face Pulls

Day 6: Rest

Day 7: Rest

For each exercise, aim for 3 sets of 8-12 reps. For cardio, aim for a moderate intensity where you can talk but not sing. Remember to start with light weights and focus on your form. Gradually increase the weights as you get stronger. Always warm up before starting your workout and cool down afterwards.
```

This example demonstrates how you can interact with ChatGPT iteratively, refining the output until you get the desired result. It is important to provide as much relevant information as possible in your prompts and to be specific about what you are asking for.

C. Exercises

Write prompts asking ChatGPT:
• To generate a workout plan for a specific goal.
• To create a 7-day diet plan for a specific dietary need.
• For the key points to include in a fitness goal for a specific type of exercise.
• For a comparison of two fitness products based on the best criteria it can generate.
• For ideas on fitness routine for different members of your family.

D. Summary

In this chapter, we have explored how ChatGPT can enrich your fitness practice, from creating workouts and diet tips to goal setting and collaboration. Yet, it is essential to remember it is not a professional advice substitute, necessitating content verification and adherence to fitness industry best practices.

SECTION 3: Extending the Power of ChatGPT

Harness and extend the power of ChatGPT – Advanced Topics

29. ChatGPT for Programmers

ChatGPT's training data also included a large amount of coding data across different programming languages. OpenAI has fine-tuned it further over time for coding. As a result, ChatGPT can produce near flawless code in several programming languages and it is already proving to be a game-changer for programmers.

This chapter will guide you with some basic examples on how to leverage the power of AI to assist with code generation, debugging and learning new programming languages. Please note that while ChatGPT can be a valuable tool, it is not a substitute for professional programming practices. Always verify and test the code provided by ChatGPT and follow best practices in programming.

A. Few Ideas and Examples

1. Code Generation

ChatGPT can be a valuable tool for generating code snippets. By providing it with a specific task, a programming narrative (pseudo code) or a set of parameters, it can generate a piece of code that performs the desired task.

Example: Suppose you are writing a Python function to calculate the factorial of a number. You might prompt ChatGPT with something like, "Write a Python function to calculate the factorial of a number.”. ChatGPT could then provide a Python function that calculates the factorial of a number.

2. Debugging

ChatGPT can assist in debugging code by suggesting potential causes for errors and possible solutions. It can provide insights into error messages and suggest changes to fix the errors.

Example: If you are debugging a piece of code and encounter an error message, you might ask ChatGPT, "What does this error message mean and how can I fix it?”. ChatGPT could provide an explanation of the error message and suggest potential solutions.

3. Learning New Programming Languages

ChatGPT can aid in learning new programming languages by providing explanations of syntax, demonstrating how to perform specific tasks, and generating practice exercises.

Example: If you are learning JavaScript and want to understand how to use the map function, you could ask ChatGPT, "Explain how to use the map function in JavaScript and provide an example.". ChatGPT might provide an explanation of the map function and an example of its use.

4. Collaboration

ChatGPT can help foster effective collaboration by generating clear and concise code comments, assisting in code reviews, and suggesting best practices for collaboration in programming.

Example: If you are working on a collaborative programming project and need to write clear code comments, you could ask ChatGPT, "What are some best practices for writing clear and effective code comments?". ChatGPT might provide a list of best practices for writing code comments.

5. Other Examples

- Test case generation
- Conversion of code between different programming languages
- Identifying software vulnerabilities

- API usage examples
- Translating technical requirements into code

The possibilities are endless.

B. Applied Example: Debugging

Here is a detailed simulation of how a user might interact with ChatGPT to debug a piece of code. Let's say you are working on a Python script and encounter an error. Here is how you might interact with ChatGPT:

```
User: I'm getting a "TypeError: unsupported operand type(s) for +: 'int' and 'str'" error in my Python script. What does this error mean and how can I fix it?

ChatGPT: This error typically occurs when you're trying to concatenate or add an integer and a string in Python, which is not allowed. Python doesn't know how to interpret this operation because it's not clear whether you want to perform arithmetic addition (which is not possible with a string and an integer) or string concatenation (which requires both operands to be strings).

To fix this error, you need to make sure that both operands are of the same type. If you want to perform arithmetic addition, both operands should be numbers (integers or floats). If you want to concatenate strings, both operands should be strings.
```

Here's an example of how to fix this error:

If your code looks like this:

```
age = 25
message = "Happy " + age + "th Birthday!"
print(message)
```

You're trying to concatenate a string ("Happy ") with an integer (age), and then another string ("th Birthday!"). This will result in a TypeError. To fix this, you can convert the integer to a string using the str() function:

```
age = 25
message = "Happy " + str(age) + "th Birthday!"
print(message)
```

Now, the age is converted to a string before it's concatenated with the other strings, and the code will run without errors.

This simple example demonstrates how you can interact with ChatGPT iteratively, refining the output until you get the desired result. It is important to provide as much relevant information as possible in your prompts and to be specific about what you are asking for.

C. Exercises

Write prompts asking ChatGPT:

- To generate a piece of code for a specific task.

Write prompts asking ChatGPT:
• To explain an error message and suggest a solution.
• To explain a concept in a programming language.
• For best practices in collaborative programming.
• To convert a python program to javascript.

D. Summary

In this chapter, we have explored the various ways ChatGPT can assist programmers. From generating code and assisting with debugging, to aiding in learning new programming languages and fostering effective collaboration, ChatGPT can be a valuable tool in your programming practice. Always verify the code provided by ChatGPT and follow best practices in programming.

30. Integrating ChatGPT using APIs

An API, or Application Programming Interface, is a set of rules that allows different software applications to communicate with each other. The OpenAI API provides a way to interact with ChatGPT programmatically, which means you can integrate ChatGPT into your own applications, websites, or services. The API allows you to send prompts to ChatGPT and receive responses, among other things.

In the ever-evolving landscape of artificial intelligence, the integration of ChatGPT using OpenAI APIs has opened up exciting possibilities for creating innovative conversational applications. In this chapter I will explore the process of using OpenAI APIs to seamlessly integrate ChatGPT into your own applications or computer programs.

By following the steps outlined here, you can harness the power of ChatGPT to provide personalized assistance, engage in meaningful conversations, and deliver valuable insights to your application users.

More information and help can be found at **https://platform.openai.com/docs/api-reference/introduction**

A. Setting Up OpenAI API Access

Before integrating ChatGPT into your programs or applications, you will need to set up the necessary access to OpenAI APIs.

On a slightly technical note: You can interact with the OpenAI API through HTTP requests from any programming language. For this you can use OpenAI's official Python bindings, their Node.js library, or other community-maintained libraries.

Here are the steps to setup OpenAI API access.

1. Obtain OpenAI API Key

Sign up for an OpenAI account and generate an API key at **https://platform.openai.com/account/api-keys**. The process is very straightforward. This key serves as your authentication token for accessing OpenAI APIs securely.

Costs may be incurred using an OpenAI API key. Please check OpenAI documentation for more information on costs for accessing different language models.

2. Install OpenAI Python Library

Install the OpenAI Python library, which provides convenient functions for interacting with OpenAI APIs. You can use pip or another package manager to install the library in your development environment.

3. Configure API Authentication

Configure your application to use your API key for authentication when making requests to OpenAI APIs. This ensures that your requests are properly authorized and associated with your account.

B. Creating a ChatGPT Integration

Once you have set up the necessary API access, you can begin integrating ChatGPT into your applications. The following steps outline the process.

1. Design the scenarios of integration with ChatGPT

Assuming you have planned and architected your application, plan all the scenarios and use cases where you wish to integrate ChatGPT. You may choose to code your application first without ChatGPT integration or with simulated integration and later replace your simulations with real integration.

2. Initialize ChatGPT

Use the OpenAI Python library to initialize a ChatGPT instance, providing your API key as a parameter. This step establishes the connection between your application and the OpenAI infrastructure.

3. Craft User Prompts

User prompts serve as inputs to ChatGPT, guiding its responses. Craft well-structured prompts or user prompt handlers in your application to ensure effective communication with ChatGPT. Consider the context, desired outcomes, and user expectations when constructing prompts.

4. Send User Queries

Pass user prompts or reformatted user prompts per your application design (for predictable application performance) as input to ChatGPT using the initialized instance. Utilize the library functions to send queries and receive responses from ChatGPT in a conversational manner.

5. Process end to end integration and test

You can now code and complete all your integration scenarios end to end. Incorporate additional context or user-specific information to enhance the quality of interactions as desired or per the function of your program/application.

C. Few Ideas and Examples

Now, let's explore some practical applications where you can leverage ChatGPT's integration using OpenAI APIs. These examples illustrate the versatility and potential of incorporating ChatGPT into your applications:

1. Virtual Personal Assistant

A virtual personal assistant that leverages ChatGPT to provide personalized assistance, answer queries, and perform tasks based on user prompts. For instance, users could ask for reminders, schedule management, weather updates, or recommendations for nearby restaurants.

2. Customer Support Chatbot

A customer support chatbot that integrates ChatGPT to handle customer queries and provide instant responses. The chatbot could assist with product information, troubleshooting, and common inquiries, enhancing customer service efficiency.

3. Language Learning App

A language learning app that utilizes ChatGPT to offer interactive language practice sessions. Users can engage in conversations with ChatGPT, practicing their speaking and comprehension skills while receiving feedback and guidance.

4. Content Generation Tool

A content generation tool that utilizes ChatGPT to assist with writing tasks. Users can provide prompts related to blog articles, essays, or creative writing, and ChatGPT can generate relevant content to streamline the writing process.

5. Other Applications

- Writing assistants or content editors
- Legal research and analysis tools
- Personal finance and budgeting apps
- Interactive storytelling or narrative generation
- Travel planning and recommendation apps

The possibilities are endless.

D. Applied Example: Content Generation Tool

Here is an example skeleton code that can be part of a simple Content Generation tool that I described earlier.

This skeleton code provides an example for the basic structure for initializing ChatGPT, generating content iteratively, and extracting the final generated content. You can customize the code by adding additional logic, error handling, and any necessary pre-processing and post-processing steps to enhance the functionality of your content generation app. Remember to replace 'YOUR_API_KEY' with your actual OpenAI API key. In doing so, remember to manage API usage costs well.

This is a simplified example, and you may need to modify it based on your specific requirements and programming environment.

```
import openai

# Set up OpenAI API credentials
openai.api_key = 'YOUR_API_KEY'

# Function to initialize ChatGPT
def initialize_chatgpt():
    # Initialize and configure ChatGPT instance
    chatgpt = openai.ChatCompletion.create(
        model="gpt-3.5-turbo",
        messages=[
            {"role": "system", "content": "You
are a helpful assistant."},
            {"role": "user", "content": "Hi, I
need assistance with content generation."},
        ]
    )
    return chatgpt

# Function to generate content
def generate_content(prompt):
```

```
        # Initialize ChatGPT
        chatgpt = initialize_chatgpt()

        # Create conversation history with user
prompt
        conversation = [
            {"role": "user", "content": prompt}
        ]

        # Generate content iteratively
        while True:
            # Generate response from ChatGPT
            response = openai.ChatCompletion.create(
                model="gpt-3.5-turbo",
                messages=conversation
            )

            # Get the model's reply
            reply =
response.choices[0].message.content

            # Add user input and model reply to the
conversation
            conversation.append({"role": "user",
"content": reply})

            # Check if the content generation is
complete
```

```
            if is_content_complete(reply):
                break

        # Extract the generated content
        generated_content =
extract_generated_content(conversation)

        return generated_content

    # Function to check if content generation is
complete
    def is_content_complete(reply):
        # Implement your logic here
        # For example, you can define certain
keywords that indicate completion

    # Function to extract the generated content from
conversation history
    def extract_generated_content(conversation):
        # Implement your logic here
        # Extract the desired content from the
conversation history

    # Main function
    def main():
        # Prompt the user for content generation
        prompt = input("Enter your content generation
prompt: ")
```

```
        # Generate content
        generated_content = generate_content(prompt)

        # Print the generated content
        print("Generated Content:")
        print(generated_content)

# Run the main function
if __name__ == "__main__":
    main()
```

E. Ethical Considerations and Best Practices

Integrating ChatGPT with OpenAI APIs brings immense potential, but it is important to be aware of ethical considerations and best practices. Here are some suggestions. Please ensure you consider additional criteria depending on the use case of your application.

1. User Privacy

Respect user privacy and ensure that any personal information provided by users is handled securely and in compliance with relevant regulations.

2. Consent

If user data is being used or shared in any way, it is important to ensure that users have given their informed consent. Consider implementing a robust consent management process in your application, especially when integrating with third-party capabilities, to understand dependencies and how they may impact your own responsibilities.

3. Bias Mitigation

Be mindful of potential biases in ChatGPT's responses and implement techniques to mitigate them. Consider pre-processing inputs, providing context, or employing post-processing measures to deliver fair and unbiased interactions.

4. User Empowerment

Empower users by clearly indicating when they are interacting with an AI and allowing them to control the level of AI involvement in their interactions. Transparency, coupled with user consent, is paramount.

5. Content Moderation

Implement robust content moderation mechanisms to prevent misuse or dissemination of inappropriate, harmful, or misleading information through your application.

6. Accessibility

This is one of the most overlooked aspects by application developers. However, as AI becomes more integrated into our lives, it is doubly important to ensure that these technologies are accessible to all, regardless of their technical skills or abilities. Regardless of AI, I recommend building your applications with accessibility in mind. After all, accessible applications become more useful to any user if implemented well.

7. Security

Implement robust security handling mechanisms as you integrate your applications and programs with third-party applications. When integrating with third-party applications, it is important to ensure that these tools are secure and do not pose a risk to user data.

8. Accountability

As AI systems become more integrated and are used in more critical applications, it is important to have clear lines of accountability for when things go wrong. In your application design, plan for thorough management of accountability so that you can manage risks more effectively.

9. Plan for AI Hallucinations

As I mentioned in the Foreword, Language Models like ChatGPT can sometimes generate inaccurate or false information, known as 'hallucinations'. If you are in full control of the prompt engineering in your applications, the chances of such hallucinations should be minimal. However, implement robust checks, balances, and safety mechanisms in your application to prevent unintended consequences or harm due to this potential. This will especially be important if your application uses free-form text inputs from users.

F. Summary

In this chapter, we explored the process of integrating ChatGPT with OpenAI APIs to enhance your applications with enhanced conversational capabilities. You can create virtual assistants, chatbots, language learning apps, and content generation tools that deliver exceptional user experiences. Remember to adhere to ethical guidelines and best practices. Iterate and improve your application continuously to provide valuable and responsible AI-driven interactions.

As the integration of ChatGPT with OpenAI APIs continues to evolve, it opens up a world of possibilities for creating innovative applications that leverage the power of conversational AI. Embrace this opportunity to create user-centric solutions that redefine the way we interact with technology and unlock new levels of productivity and engagement.

31. Extending ChatGPT with Web Browsing

The recent ability of ChatGPT (available to ChatGPT Plus users currently) to browse the web has opened up a new frontier in the realm of artificial intelligence. This enhancement allows ChatGPT to pull in current information from the web, making it an even more powerful tool for research, fact-checking, and staying up-to-date with the latest news and events. This chapter will explore how to leverage this new capability, with a focus on its applications in various fields.

Please note that while ChatGPT's web browsing capability provides access to a vast amount of information, it is essential to remember that not all information on the web is accurate or reliable. Always cross-verify the information provided by ChatGPT with other reliable sources.

A. Accessing Web Browsing for ChatGPT

As we learnt in Section 1, available to ChatGPT Plus users, if you select GPT-4 (or the latest model available), you can use the advanced features like extending ChatGPT with Web browsing capabilities.

To enable web browsing for a particular chat, simple select "Browse with Bing" at the start of your chat. ChatGPT will either automatically access the web if needed or you can ask it to access the web or a URL explicitly.

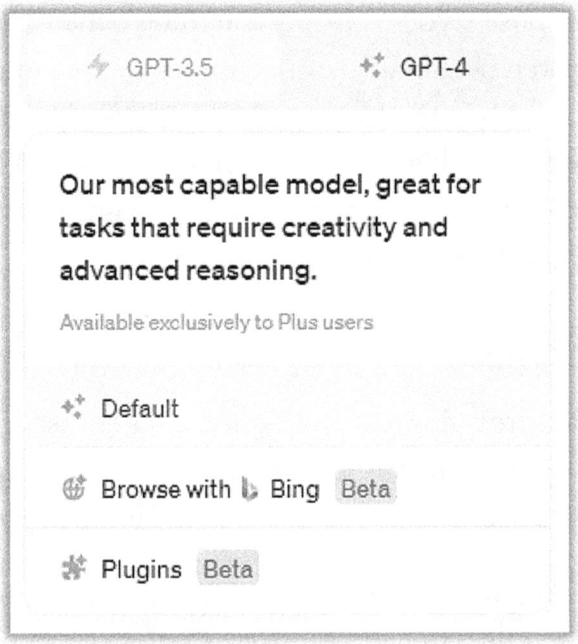

As the time of writing of this book, this feature was in Beta (experimental) stage and OpenAI was in the process of refining it.

B. Few Ideas and Examples

1. Research

With web browsing capabilities, ChatGPT can now pull in the most recent information available on the web. This makes it a powerful tool for conducting research on a wide range of topics.

Example: Suppose you are researching the latest developments in renewable energy technology. You might prompt ChatGPT with something like, "What are the latest advancements in renewable energy technology?". ChatGPT could then browse the web to find the most recent articles, research papers, and news reports on the topic.

2. Fact-Checking

ChatGPT's web browsing capability can also be used for fact-checking. It can pull in information from reliable sources to verify the accuracy of a statement or piece of information.

Example: If you come across a statement claiming that a particular country is the largest producer of solar energy, you could ask ChatGPT, "Which country is currently the largest producer of solar energy?". ChatGPT would then browse the web to find the most recent and reliable data on the topic.

3. Current Events

ChatGPT can now provide information on the latest news and current events by browsing the web.

Example: If you want to know the latest news about the stock market, you could ask ChatGPT, "What's the latest news about stock X?". ChatGPT would then browse the web to find the most recent news articles on the topic.

4. Miscellaneous Applications

The web browsing capability of ChatGPT can be used in numerous other ways, such as finding recipes, checking weather forecasts, finding local businesses, comparing products, summarizing blog articles and much more.

Example: If you are planning a trip and want to know the weather for your destination, you could ask ChatGPT, "What's the weather forecast for Paris next week?". ChatGPT would then browse the web to find the recent forecasts.

5. Other Examples

- Product Comparisons
- Real-Time Data Analysis
- Personalized Learning from web content
- Job Hunting
- Personal Shopping recommendations

The possibilities are endless.

C. Applied Example: Web Research

Here is a detailed simulation of how a user might interact with ChatGPT to conduct research on a specific topic. Let's say you are writing a report on the impact of climate change on agriculture. Here is how you might interact with ChatGPT:

User: I'm writing a report on the impact of climate change on agriculture. Can you help me find the latest research on this topic?

ChatGPT: Absolutely! I can browse the web to find the most recent research papers, articles, and reports on the impact of climate change on agriculture. Please wait a moment while I gather this information.

[*ChatGPT then browses the web and returns with a list of recent research papers, articles, and reports on the topic, along with brief summaries of each source.*]

This example demonstrates how you can use ChatGPT's web browsing capability to conduct research on a specific topic. Remember to always cross-verify the information provided by ChatGPT with other reliable sources.

D. Exercises

Write prompts asking ChatGPT to:

- Review and compare the two recent balance sheets of a public company.

Write prompts asking ChatGPT to:
• Find the latest research on a topic of your choice.
• Find the latest news on a specific topic.
• Compare two products on certain criteria, while providing the public links to the product detail pages.
• To summarize a blog article. You will provide the public link to the blog article.

E. Summary

In this chapter, we have explored the various ways you can leverage ChatGPT's web browsing capability. From conducting research and fact-checking to staying up-to-date with current events, this new feature significantly enhances the utility of ChatGPT. However, it is essential to remember that not all information on the web is accurate or reliable. Always cross-verify the information provided by ChatGPT with other reliable sources.

32. Extending ChatGPT with Plugins

A plugin can be described as a software component that adds a specific feature or functionality to an existing application. In the case of ChatGPT, plugins offer ways to extend and diversify the capabilities of the language model.

Plugins are a new and the most exciting addition to ChatGPT's capabilities. This has created tremendous interest among users and developers due to its capacity to significantly widen the scope to virtually limitless possible applications for ChatGPT.

At the time of writing of this book, OpenAI has confined the roll-out of plugins to ChatGPT Plus subscribers. The aim seems to gradually increase access as OpenAI gains more insights into the utilization. This will eventually extend to API users who wish to integrate ChatGPT connected to these plugins into their own products. This approach is in line with OpenAI's iterative approach to their model deployment, progressively introducing new features to evaluate their safety, real-world usage, impact, and potential challenges.

The first series of plugins have been created by various contributors, including Expedia, Instacart, KAYAK, OpenTable, Shopify, Slack, Wolfram, Zapier etc. More plugins are being rolled out almost every week. These initial plugins mark an important milestone in the ongoing development of ChatGPT and its interaction paradigm with human users.

In this chapter I will only touch on the usage of plugins for ChatGPT. Creating plugins is outside the scope of this book. However, if you are inclined, OpenAI provides comprehensive documentation on how to build and publish plugins for ChatGPT.

A. How Plugins for ChatGPT Work

Plugins provide a bridge between ChatGPT and external applications. Plugin developers reveal one or more APIs, a uniform manifest file[8] and an OpenAPI[9] specification. These outline the plugin's functionality, enabling ChatGPT to

[8] In simple terms, a manifest file is like a table of contents or an instruction manual for a software program. It provides important information about the different components of the program, such as files, resources, and settings. This information helps a system to understand how to handle the program correctly. For example, it might tell the system what permissions the program needs, what version of the software it is, or what other programs or libraries it depends on to function properly.

[9] The OpenAPI Specification (OAS) is a standard for defining APIs

interpret the files and interact with the APIs defined by the developer. Consider this as the plugin's blueprint.

Think of the plugin scenario as the opposite of OpenAI APIs scenario that you learned about in the earlier chapter. Instead of an external program calling ChatGPT, ChatGPT calls an external program/application.

The beauty of this is, due to its access to the installed plugins' API blueprints, ChatGPT intelligently decides to interact with the correct plugin to execute tasks - only if needed. For example, if a user inquires, "What's a good place to stay in New York for a few days?", ChatGPT may opt to engage a hotel booking plugin's API, process the returned data, and formulate a response in everyday language for the user.

These plugins can broaden ChatGPT's abilities and facilitate infinite array of functions. For example, plugins may equip ChatGPT to perform tasks such as:

- Fetching live data; for instance, updates on current events, stock market trends, weather and so forth.
- Help with performing actual tasks; for instance, making travel reservations, ordering online products, food delivery, and so forth.
- Accessing data from a given knowledge-base; for instance, from documents, websites, notes, and so forth.

- Connect with Other API services; for instance, consider the special scenario of a plugin from Zapier (a separate Zapier account required subject to Zapier's' terms and conditions) which in itself provides bridges to thousands of other applications. Imagine the endless possibilities!

B. Using Plugins

From an end user perspective, plugins can be accessed from the ChatGPT Plus interface. Here is an outline of how to access and use Plugins.

1. Enable the desired plugin(s)

In the ChatGPT Plus interface, click on GPT-4 (at the time of writing this book. This may change to GPT-5 and so on) and select/click on Plugins

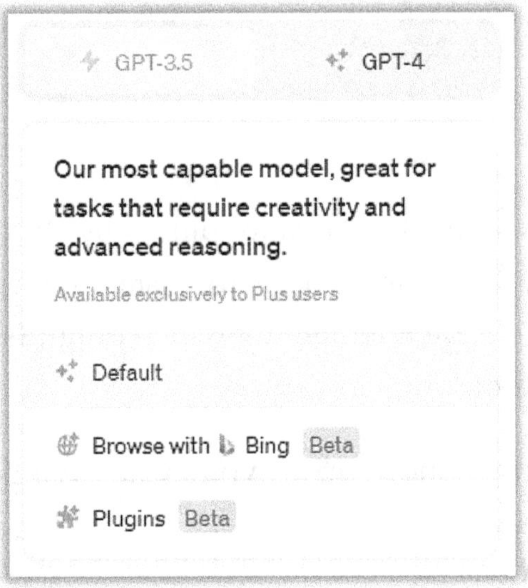

2. Install the Plugin(s)

Access the plugin store by clicking on the drop down labeled "No Plugins enabled" which shows up after step 1.

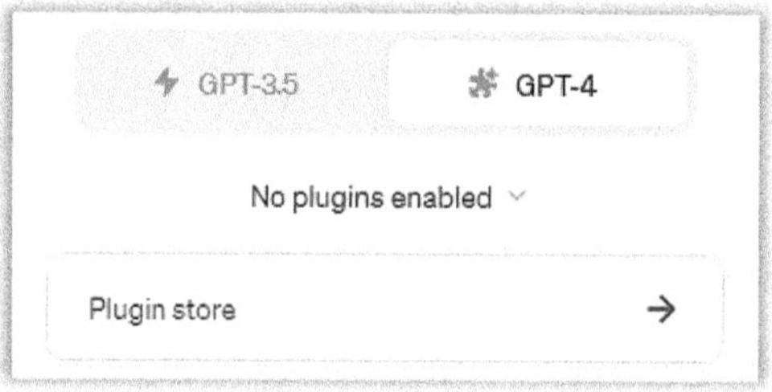

This will open the Plugin Store

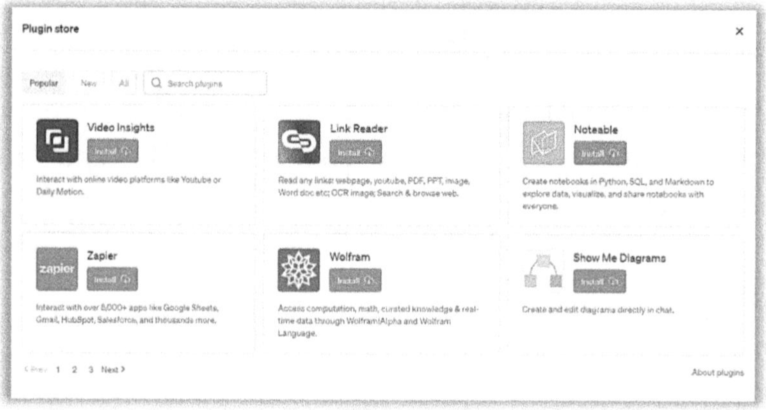

For example, lets install the Link Reader plugin by clicking on the Install button. You can choose to install multiple plugins. ChatGPT will decide intelligently which plugin(s) to use based on your prompt.

The plugin(s) will now show up in your Chat Window under the Model selection.

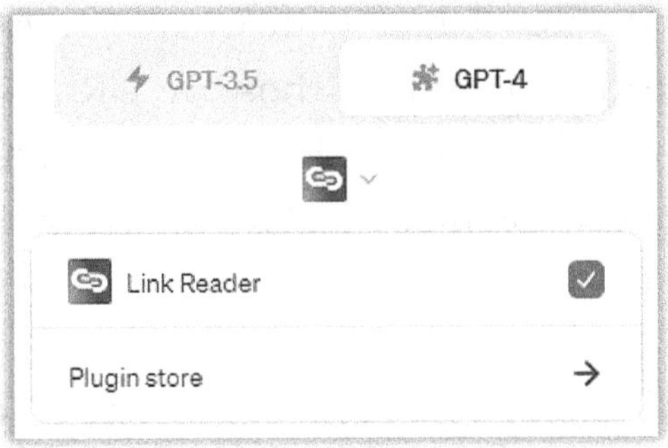

You can install multiple plugins for your chats. Once you start a chat session and would like to add a new plugin, you will need to start a new chat. The earlier plugins that you installed will be available in the new chat. For example,

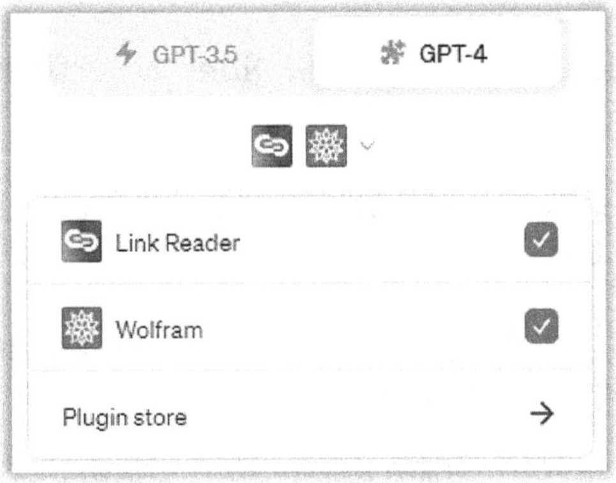

You can disable or re-enable an installed plugin for a chat by unchecking it from the list of installed plugins before you start the chat.

3. Use the Plugin

ChatGPT will automatically start using relevant plugin(s) based on your prompt. For example, let's consider the following real interaction that I had with ChatGPT. After installing the Link Reader plugin, I chose a URL with information from the year 2022 which is after the training cutoff date for the current version of ChatGPT at the time of writing of this book.

```
User: Hi, can you please review the content on the following webpage and provide me a 10-bullet summary with each bullet less than 20 words? https://en.wikipedia.org/wiki/2022_in_the_United_States

ChatGPT: Here is a 10-point summary of the events in the United States in 2022, each bullet is less than 20 words:

1. Supreme Court overturned Roe v. Wade, sparking nationwide protests.

2. Labor unions gained traction, targeting Apple, Starbucks, and Amazon.

3. Economy impacted by global inflation surge, stock market decline, and gas price increase.

4. Federal Reserve implemented aggressive interest rate hikes, reaching 4.4% by year's end.

5. Tech industry saw major acquisitions, including Elon Musk's acquisition of Twitter.

6. Midterm elections held on November 8, deciding numerous state and local elections.
```

```
   7. Democratic Party maintained Senate lead;
Republican Party retook the House of
Representatives.

   8. First female governors elected in Arkansas,
Massachusetts, and New York.

   9. San Francisco District Attorney Chesa Boudin
successfully recalled and ousted.

   10. Significant events included Supreme Court
nomination of Judge Ketanji Brown Jackson.
```

At the top of the interaction, ChatGPT will show drop down(s) for the plugin(s) it used to provide the response. In this example, it shows Used Link Reader drop down.

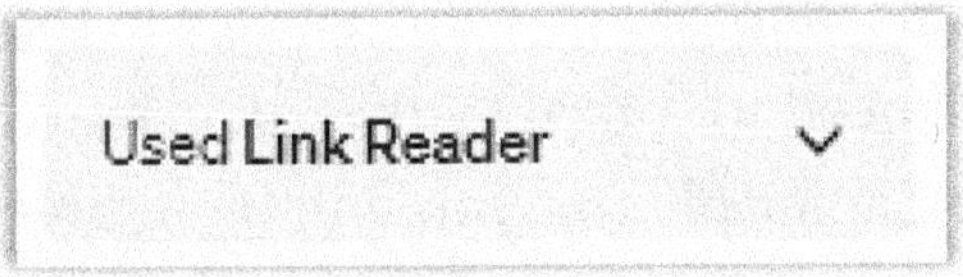

Expanding the dropdown shows the actual data exchange between ChatGPT and the plugin.

4. Uninstalling plugin(s)

To uninstall a plugin, you can simply navigate to the Plugin store and click on Uninstall as below. However, if you just want to avoid the usage of a plugin for a chat, you can simply disable it for a chat, as I described earlier.

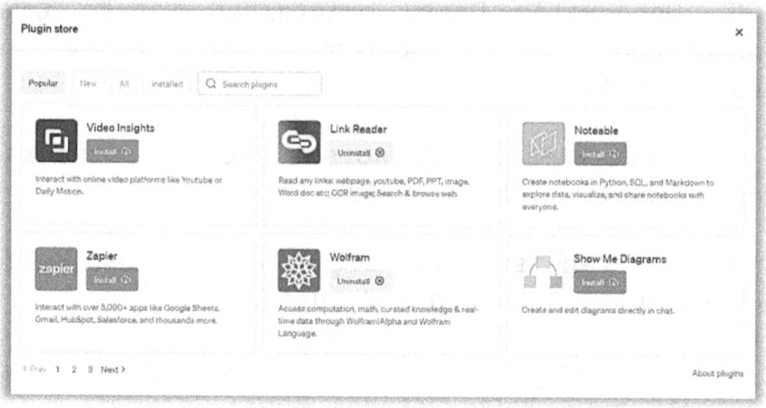

C. Plugin Usage Considerations

Some plugins will require you to have an account with the plugin creator which may be a paid account and may have its own terms and conditions (and of any third parties in use by the plugin) that you will need to comply with. For example, if you chose to install the Zapier plugin, you will be redirected to the Zapier website to login to your account. Once you successfully do that, you will be able to install the plugin and use it with ChatGPT.

The key limitations of ChatGPT that I have pointed out in this book and any other that OpenAI has cited will still apply when you use plugins. Furthermore, there may be limitations of the plugins as well. It is essential to understand these limitations when interacting with ChatGPT with plugins as well, and to verify any critical information it provides via the plugins, especially in high precision fields such as medical or legal advice.

D. Exercises

- Install various plugins and experiment with ChatGPT's responses. Verify the responses by manual research.
- Install a Travel service plugin like e.g., Expedia and prompt ChatGPT to help plan your trip budget with available prices for your trip dates.
- Install a Scientific research plugin like e.g., ScholarAI and prompt ChatGPT to review several related research papers and provide you a summary.
- Install a pdf reader plugin e.g., ChatWithPDF. Provide ChatGPT a URL to a publicly available pdf book and conduct a chat around the details in the pdf. Try it with your own pdfs as long as you can provide a public URL.
- Explore creating your own ChatGPT plugin.

E. Summary

In summary, this final chapter reviews the concept of plugins for ChatGPT, a transformative feature that significantly enhances the language model's capabilities. Plugins, created by various contributors, act as bridges between ChatGPT and external applications, allowing the model to perform a wide range of tasks.

Some plugins may require users to have an account with the plugin creator, which may be a paid account and may have its own terms and conditions. The limitations of ChatGPT and the plugins themselves are also important to consider.

As we close this last chapter, it is my hope that you now feel empowered with a demystified understanding of ChatGPT. You have journeyed through the intricacies of this language model, learned how to craft effective prompts, understood the differences between various platforms, and now, you have grasped the transformative potential of plugins. With this knowledge, you are equipped to harness the power of ChatGPT to improve your life, boost your productivity, and explore new frontiers of possibility.

The journey with ChatGPT does not end here. As you continue to interact with this powerful tool, you will discover new ways to use it, and perhaps, even contribute to its evolution!

CONCLUSION

33. Conclusion

Congratulations! You have journeyed through the fascinating world of ChatGPT, exploring its capabilities and applications, and unlocking its potential to transform your life.

Isn't it amazing to think about how much you can do with ChatGPT? From drafting an impressive business proposal to brainstorming the plot of your next novel, or assisting with your child's homework to creating your business plan, ChatGPT is ready to lend a hand.

Whether you are already a ChatGPT user or about to dive in, you are embarking on an exciting journey. As you have read this book, you may have been practicing, experimenting, and discovering just how much ChatGPT can enhance your life. If you haven't started yet, there's no better time than now!

This is just the beginning. The world of AI is constantly evolving, and ChatGPT is continually learning and growing. The future may bring new features and capabilities that we can only imagine today.

You might be thinking, "Sure, this all sounds great, but some of these features require a paid version.". That is true. But consider this: the time, energy, and creativity that ChatGPT can help you unlock are priceless. The potential to multiply your productivity, ignite your creativity, and even propel you towards financial success is well worth the investment.

Are you ready to embrace the future? To harness the power of AI and step into a world of limitless possibilities? I hope this book has inspired you to do just that.

AI isn't something to fear. It is a tool, a companion, a helper in our daily lives. With ChatGPT by your side, you are not just keeping up with the times. You are riding the wave of the future, ready to seize the opportunities it brings.

So go ahead, dive in, start or continue using ChatGPT, and see where it takes you. Whether you are drafting an email, writing a story, planning a project, or just having a fun chat, remember to enjoy the journey.

After all, you are not just using a tool. You are participating in one of the most exciting technological revolutions of our time.

Here's to your future with ChatGPT. It's going to be an exciting ride!

34. Glossary

Alongside the main content of the book, I have included this comprehensive glossary. *This is not just a collection of terms used throughout the book.* It goes a step further to cover broader terminology that you will encounter when exploring the topics of artificial intelligence and ChatGPT.

My aim is to empower you with a vocabulary that not only ensures clarity and understanding as you navigate through the chapters but also helps you to engage confidently in any AI-related discussions. Knowledge is power, and understanding these terms will equip you with the necessary armor to combat any attempts at mystification or power play.

By demystifying the jargon, I hope to foster an environment where everyone, irrespective of their background, can participate in meaningful conversations about AI and its fascinating applications.

Term	Definition
AI (Artificial Intelligence)	A branch of computer science that involves the development of machines and software capable of intelligent behavior.
Algorithm	A set of rules or procedures for solving a problem or accomplishing a task, often used by a computer.
API (Application Programming Interface)	A set of rules and protocols for building and interacting with software applications.
Attention Mechanism	In the context of transformer-based models like GPT, the attention mechanism allows the model to weigh the importance of different words in the input when generating an output.
Autoregression	A type of statistical analysis where the current value is a function of previous values. In language models like GPT, it refers to predicting the next word based on the previous ones.
Backpropagation	A method used in artificial neural networks to calculate the error contribution of each neuron after a batch of data is processed.
Bias	In AI, bias refers to algorithms that systematically favor certain outcomes over others, often in a way that is unfair or discriminatory.
Chatbot	A computer program that simulates human conversation through voice commands or text chats or both.
ChatGPT	A state-of-the-art language model developed by OpenAI that uses machine learning to produce human-like text.
Completion	The term "completion" in AI can be context-dependent. In the context of conversational

Term	Definition
	AI like ChatGPT, a "completion" might be considered as a complete interaction cycle, which includes: 1. The user sending a message or input to ChatGPT. 2. ChatGPT processing the input and generating a response. 3. The user receiving the response from ChatGPT. However, the term is most commonly used to refer to the text generated by ChatGPT in response to a given input or prompt.
Context Window	The number of preceding and following words used as context in a natural language processing task.
Data Analysis	A process of inspecting, cleansing, transforming, and modeling data with the goal of discovering useful information, informing conclusions, and supporting decision-making.
Data Augmentation	Techniques used to increase the amount of training data, such as random transformations and permutations of the data.
Deep Learning	A type of machine learning that trains a computer to perform human-like tasks, such as recognizing speech, identifying images or making predictions.
Deepfake	Synthetic media e.g., text, video, audio etc. in which a person's likeness is replaced with someone else's likeness using AI.
Ecommerce	The activity of electronically buying or selling products on online services or over the Internet.

Term	Definition
Ethics	The moral principles that govern a person's behavior or the conducting of an activity. In AI, ethics involves considerations about fairness, transparency, privacy, and accountability.
Few-Shot Learning	A learning paradigm in machine learning where the aim is to design machine learning models that can learn useful information from a small number of examples – typically 1-10 examples.
Fine-tuning	A process where a pre-trained model like GPT is further trained on a specific task or dataset to adapt its knowledge to the specific task.
Generative Model	A type of AI model that is able to generate new content.
GPT (Generative Pretrained Transformer)	A model architecture that processes input data (such as a sentence) in parallel rather than sequentially, leading to more efficient learning. In other words, instead of analyzing a sentence word by word in order (like we humans usually do), it can look at all the words at once and determine how they relate to each other, which is especially useful in understanding the context of words in a sentence. In simpler terms: **Generative**: This refers to the ability of the model to create new content. In this context, "generative" means that the AI can generate, or create, text that it hasn't been explicitly programmed to produce.

Term	Definition
	Pre-trained: This term means that the model has undergone a period of "training" before it is used for its specific task. During training, the model is exposed to a large amount of data and learns patterns and structures in this data. It uses this knowledge to generate relevant and coherent responses. **Transformer**: This is a type of natural language processing design used in making the AI. It is like the blueprint for a house. This design is especially good at understanding how words in a sentence relate to each other, which helps the AI generate better responses. For example, it can figure out when "bank" means a place to keep money and when it means to rely on something. This understanding of how words work together is a big part of what makes ChatGPT work well.
Hyperparameters	In machine learning, these are parameters that are set before the learning process begins, and control aspects of the learning process itself.
Language model	A type of AI model that is trained to understand and generate human language.
Loss Function	A measure of how far a machine learning model's predictions are from the true values. The goal in training these models is to minimize the loss function.

Term	Definition
Machine Learning	A type of artificial intelligence that enables computers to learn and make decisions without being explicitly programmed.
Masked Language Model	A type of language model where some words in the input are masked, and the task is to predict the masked words based on the context provided by the unmasked words. This concept is not specific to GPT but is central to other transformer models like BERT(Bidirectional Encoder Representations from Transformers).
Natural Language Processing (NLP)	A field of AI that focuses on the interaction between computers and humans through natural language.
Neural network	A computing system inspired by the human brain, composed of interconnected nodes ("neurons") that process information and learn from it.
Nodes or Neurons	In a neural network, these are the basic units of computation that receive input, process it, and pass it on.
OpenAI	OpenAI is an American artificial intelligence research laboratory and corporation. OpenAI conducts AI research with the declared intention of promoting and developing friendly AI.
Out-of-vocabulary (OOV)	Refers to words that are not included in the vocabulary of a natural language processing model.
Overfitting	In machine learning, this occurs when a model learns from both the underlying patterns and the noise in the training data, to the point where it performs poorly on unseen data.

Term	Definition
Pattern	A regular and intelligible form or sequence discernible in certain actions or situations.
Prompt	In the context of AI, a prompt is the input given to a language model, which it uses to generate a response.
Prompt Design	The overall process of constructing a prompt: determining what information to include, how to phrase the prompt, what format to use, etc., with the goal of guiding the AI to produce a specific type of response. It is often used interchangeably with Prompt Engineering.
Prompt Engineering	The process of carefully designing and testing prompts to get desirable responses from language models like GPT. It is a term that can encompass prompt design, but may also imply an iterative process of experimenting with different prompts, measuring their effectiveness, and refining them based on feedback or data. This could include testing multiple versions of prompts, analyzing the performance of different prompts, and systematically improving them over time.
Reinforcement Learning	A type of machine learning where a model learns to behave in an environment, by performing certain actions and observing the results.
Sentiment Analysis	The use of natural language processing to identify and classify sentiments within text data.
SEO (Search Engine Optimization)	The practice of increasing the quantity and quality of traffic to your website through organic search engine results.

Term	Definition
Simulation	The imitation of the operation of a real-world process or system over time.
Supervised Learning	A type of machine learning where the model is provided with labeled training data.
Temperature Parameter	In GPT, this parameter influences the randomness of the model's output. Higher values produce more random outputs, while lower values make the output more deterministic.
Tokenization	The process of splitting up text into individual elements or "tokens". Commonly used in natural language processing.
Top-k Sampling	A text generation method used in GPT where the model selects the next word from the top 'k' most likely candidates, rather than from the entire vocabulary.
Top-p Sampling (Nucleus Sampling)	A text generation method used in GPT where the model selects the next word from the smallest set of top candidates that have a cumulative probability greater than a threshold 'p'.
Transfer Learning	A research problem in machine learning that focuses on storing knowledge gained while solving one problem and applying it to a different but related problem.
Transformer Models	A type of model architecture used in machine learning, particularly in natural language processing tasks. Known for their ability to handle sequential data, irrespective of its length.
Turing Test	A test proposed by Alan Turing to judge a machine's ability to exhibit intelligent behavior indistinguishable from that of a

Term	Definition
	human. Alan Turing was a British mathematician who is considered a pioneer in computer science and was instrumental in breaking the German Enigma code during World War II
Underfitting	In machine learning, this occurs when a model is too simple and does not learn enough from the training data, leading to poor performance on both the training and unseen data.
Unsupervised Learning	A type of machine learning where the model is not provided with labeled training data and must find patterns in the input data on its own.
Use-case policy	A set of guidelines that outline how a particular technology can and cannot be used.
Zero-Shot Learning	In machine learning, it refers to the ability of a model to correctly make predictions for classes not seen during training.

35. Quiz

Understanding and application go hand-in-hand. Therefore, the comprehensive quiz below is designed not only to test your grasp of the concepts discussed in this book, but also to reinforce your holistic understanding. The questions have been tailored to span the breadth of the content, as well as to cover some key terms defined in the glossary. This quiz offers a chance for you to reflect on what you have learned, deepen your understanding, and consolidate your knowledge. I encourage you to take this opportunity to engage with the material in a more interactive and enriching way. Remember, the goal isn't simply to get the answers right, but to comprehend the concepts well.

1) What is ChatGPT?

a) A search engine developed by OpenAI
b) A language model developed by OpenAI
c) A social media platform developed by OpenAI
d) A computer developed by OpenAI

2) Does ChatGPT have a knowledge cut-off, and what does it mean?

a) No, it continually updates its knowledge from the internet
b) Yes, it means the date after which the model has no information, as it cannot access real-time data on its own
c) Yes, it means the level of complexity beyond which the model cannot understand concepts
d) No, the model's learning capacity is unlimited and it can continue acquiring knowledge indefinitely

3) What is the output of ChatGPT based on?

a) The text it was last trained on
b) The specific prompt it is given
c) The current news on the internet
d) The private data of the users

4) Is ChatGPT capable of independent thought or consciousness?

a) Yes, it is fully sentient and self-aware
b) No, it is a tool that generates responses based on patterns in the data it was trained on
c) Yes, but only to the extent programmed by its developers
d) It is currently a subject of debate among AI experts

5) Can ChatGPT generate content in languages other than English?

a) Yes, but only in European languages

b) Yes, but only in a handful of the most spoken worldwide
c) Yes, it is capable of generating content in a wide range of languages, but performance can vary
d) No, it can only generate content in English

6) How does ChatGPT generate responses?

a) By predicting the next word in a sequence
b) By randomly selecting words from a dictionary
c) By copying text from the internet
d) By translating text from another language

7) What is the OpenAI Playground?

a) A playground built by OpenAI
b) A platform to experiment with ChatGPT
c) A video game developed by OpenAI
d) A social media platform for AI enthusiasts

8) What is the difference between free and subscription modes of ChatGPT?

a) Free mode has more features
b) Subscription mode is cheaper
c) Subscription mode provides priority access, additional features and faster response times
d) There is no difference

9) What is a prompt in the context of ChatGPT?

a) A command to start ChatGPT
b) A question or statement given to ChatGPT to generate a response
c) A type of error message

d) A type of AI model

10) What is the term for the set of rules that dictate how other programs interact with ChatGPT?

a) Algorithm
b) API (Application Programming Interface)
c) Protocol
d) Schema

11) What is the term for a system of algorithms designed to recognize patterns, similar to how the human brain works?

a) Artificial Intelligence
b) Machine Learning
c) Neural Network
d) Deep Learning

12) What is the role of specificity in prompt design for ChatGPT?

a) Specific prompts are discouraged as they limit ChatGPT's responses
b) Specific prompts help in eliciting more accurate and relevant responses from ChatGPT
c) The level of specificity in a prompt has no impact on ChatGPT's responses
d) Specific prompts cause ChatGPT to malfunction

13) What is the role of context in prompt design for ChatGPT?

a) Context in prompts is discouraged as it confuses ChatGPT
b) Context in prompts helps in eliciting more accurate and relevant responses from ChatGPT
c) Context in prompts has no impact on the responses
d) Context in prompts causes ChatGPT to malfunction

14) What is the role of ambiguity in prompt design for ChatGPT?

a) Ambiguity in prompts is encouraged as it allows ChatGPT to generate creative responses
b) Ambiguity in prompts is discouraged as it can lead to vague or irrelevant responses
c) Ambiguity in prompts has no impact on ChatGPT's responses
d) Ambiguity in prompts causes ChatGPT to malfunction

15) What is the purpose of the temperature setting in the OpenAI Playground?

a) To control the randomness of ChatGPT's responses
b) To control the heating of ChatGPT's servers
c) To control the speed of ChatGPT's responses
d) To control the politeness of ChatGPT's responses

16) What is the purpose of the maximum length setting in the OpenAI Playground?

a) To control the maximum length of ChatGPT's responses
b) To control the maximum number of responses ChatGPT can generate

c) To control the maximum speed of ChatGPT's responses
d) To control the maximum politeness of ChatGPT's responses

17) What is the purpose of the frequency penalty setting in the OpenAI Playground?

a) To penalize ChatGPT for generating frequent responses
b) To control the frequency of ChatGPT's responses
c) It helps you influence how often ChatGPT uses common phrases
d) To control the speed of ChatGPT's responses

18) What is the purpose of the presence penalty setting in the OpenAI Playground?

a) It controls how much ChatGPT introduces new concepts in its responses
b) To penalize ChatGPT for being present
c) To control the presence of ChatGPT's responses
d) To control the speed of ChatGPT's responses

19) What is the purpose of the "Ethics and Responsible Use of ChatGPT" section in the book?

a) To discuss the ethical considerations when using AI
b) To provide a history of AI ethics
c) To discuss the technical details of AI ethics
d) To provide legal advice on AI ethics

20) How can ChatGPT be used in day-to-day life?

a) For translations

b) For cooking
c) For driving
d) All of the above

21) How can ChatGPT assist students?

a) By providing research assistance
b) By helping with essay writing
c) By creating study guides
d) All of the above

22) How can ChatGPT assist lawyers?

a) By representing clients in court
b) By taking the bar exam
c) By assisting in legal research, drafting legal documents, and providing negotiation strategies
d) By providing legal advice

23) How can ChatGPT assist in the field of history?

a) By assisting in gathering historical information, providing context, and generating timelines
b) By traveling back in time
c) By playing the role of historical characters
d) By conducting archaeological reviews

24) How can ChatGPT assist in the field of real estate?

a) By buying and selling properties
b) By providing financial aid
c) By generating property descriptions, assisting in market analysis, and providing negotiation strategies
d) By conducting property inspections

25) How can ChatGPT assist in the field of programming?

a) By fixing hardware issues
b) By writing flawless computer programs
c) By assisting in code generation, debugging, and providing programming tips and resources
d) By designing software

26) How can ChatGPT assist in the field of data analysis?

a) By collecting data
b) By creating more data
c) By summarizing and interpreting data, generating insights, and recommendations
d) By conducting surveys

27) What is supervised learning in the context of AI?

a) A type of AI that involves machines learning under the supervision of humans
b) A type of AI that involves machines learning under the supervision of other machines
c) A type of AI that involves machines learning under the supervision of teachers
d) A type of AI that involves machines learning under the supervision of supervisors

28) What is a dataset in the context of AI?

a) A set of data used to train an AI model
b) A set of data used to test an AI model
c) A set of data used to validate an AI model
d) All of the above

29) What is a neural network in the context of AI??

a) A network of neurons in the human brain
b) A network of neurons in an AI model
c) A network of neurons in a computer
d) A network of neurons in the internet

30) How can ChatGPT assist in the field of scientific research?

a) By summarizing research papers
b) By generating hypotheses
c) By providing analysis of data
d) All of the above

31) What is a potential misuse of ChatGPT by a user?

a) Generating harmful or biased content
b) Generating deceptive or misleading content
c) Violating privacy or confidentiality
d) All of the above

32) What is a limitation of ChatGPT?

a) It may generate incorrect or nonsensical responses
b) It may not ask clarifying questions for ambiguous prompts
c) It may be sensitive to slight changes in input phrasing
d) All of the above

33) What is one way ChatGPT can assist in browsing the web?

a) By physically browsing the web on a computer.
b) By providing medical advice.
c) By providing legal advice.

d) By generating summaries of web content and answering questions based on the information found online.

34) What is the primary function of ChatGPT?

a) To predict stock market trends
b) To play chess
c) To understand and generate human-like text
d) To create visual art

35) How can ChatGPT assist entrepreneurs?

a) By generating business ideas
b) By creating marketing copy
c) By drafting business plans
d) All of the above

36) How can ChatGPT assist in debugging code?

a) By rewriting the entire code to avoid potential bugs.
b) By guessing the potential causes of errors without any context or error message.
c) By suggesting potential causes for errors and possible solutions based on error messages.
d) By fixing bugs automatically without any programmer intervention.

37) What is a key point to remember when using ChatGPT in your programming practice?

a) ChatGPT is always correct and does not require code verification.
b) ChatGPT can handle any programming task, regardless of its complexity.

c) Always verify and test the code provided by ChatGPT and follow best practices in programming.
d) It is safe to deploy code generated by ChatGPT directly to production without testing.

38) What is fine-tuning in the context of ChatGPT?

a) Adjusting the physical components of the AI
b) Customizing the AI's responses
c) Training the AI on specific tasks or domains
d) Improving the AI's speed

39) What is the purpose of an API key when accessing OpenAI's API?

a) It serves as a password to access all of OpenAI's resources
b) It helps in identifying the user in the OpenAI's database
c) It acts as an authentication token for accessing OpenAI APIs securely
d) It helps in tracking the usage of the OpenAI API

40) What is the initial step in integrating ChatGPT into your applications?

a) Sending user queries
b) Installing the OpenAI Python Library
c) Configuring API Authentication
d) Designing the scenarios of integration with ChatGPT

41) What are some practical applications where you can integrate ChatGPT using OpenAI APIs?

a) Virtual Personal Assistant

b) Customer Support Chatbot
c) Language Learning App
d) All of the above

42) What are some ethical considerations and best practices when integrating ChatGPT with OpenAI APIs?

a) User Privacy
b) Bias Mitigation
c) User Empowerment
d) All of the above

43) Why is planning for AI hallucinations important when integrating ChatGPT in an application?

a) Because AI can generate inaccurate or false information
b) Because AI can forget previous interactions
c) Because AI can modify the user data
d) Because AI can overload the server with information

44) What is the benefit of integrating ChatGPT with applications using OpenAI APIs?

a) It enhances applications with enhanced conversational capabilities
b) It makes the applications look more sophisticated
c) It reduces the size of the application
d) It automatically updates the applications

45) What are the steps for setting up OpenAI API access?

a) Design the scenarios of integration with ChatGPT
b) Initialize ChatGPT

c) Obtain OpenAI API Key, Install OpenAI Python Library, Configure API Authentication
d) Craft User Prompts, Send User Queries, Process end to end integration and test

46) What is a plugin in the context of ChatGPT?

a) A software component that adds features or functionality to ChatGPT.
b) A hardware accessory for ChatGPT.
c) An additional language model trained by OpenAI.
d) A standalone application that works independently from ChatGPT.

47) What is the purpose of the manifest file and OpenAPI specification in a ChatGPT plugin?

a) They outline the plugin's functionality, enabling ChatGPT to interact with the APIs defined by the developer.
b) They provide the source code for the plugin.
c) They are used to install the plugin into ChatGPT.
d) They are used to debug the plugin.

48) What does ChatGPT do if you install multiple plugins?

a) ChatGPT gets confused and does not use any of them.
b) ChatGPT uses them all at the same time.
c) ChatGPT intelligently decides which plugin to use based on your prompt.
d) ChatGPT randomly chooses a plugin to use.

49) What may some plugins require you to have in order to use them?

a) A high-speed internet connection.
b) A top-of-the-line computer.
c) An account with the plugin creator.
d) A PhD in computer science.

50) Despite the addition of plugins, what should you still be mindful of when using ChatGPT?

a) The limitations of ChatGPT and the plugin themselves.
b) The fact that you might need to install additional software to use the plugin.
c) The need to manually select the plugin each time you start a chat.
a) The risk that the plugin might become sentient and take over your computer.

A. Quiz Answers

Question	Answer	Question	Answer
1	b	26	c
2	b	27	a
3	a	28	a
4	b	29	b
5	c	30	d
6	a	31	d
7	b	32	d
8	c	33	d
9	b	34	c
10	b	35	d
11	c	36	c
12	b	37	c
13	b	38	c
14	b	39	c
15	a	40	b
16	a	41	d
17	c	42	d
18	a	43	a
19	a	44	a
20	a	45	c
21	d	46	a
22	c	47	a
23	a	48	c
24	c	49	c
25	c	50	a

Acknowledgements

I would like to express my heartfelt gratitude to the countless innovators and pioneers in the field of artificial intelligence, both past and present. Their passion, dedication, and tireless work have revolutionized how we interact with technology and understand the world. This book could not exist without their monumental contributions and the foundations they have established.

Special acknowledgement goes to OpenAI for its significant role in accelerating the progress of AI technology. The innovative work of OpenAI has democratized the power of AI, making it more accessible and beneficial to people worldwide. This book is inspired by the breakthroughs and the ethos of OpenAI, and I am truly grateful for their commitment to advancing AI in a manner that is safe and beneficial for all of humanity.

Last but certainly not least, I wish to express my deepest appreciation to my family: Neelu, Deiptii, Nisha, Vandana, Nicholas, and Alexandra. In particular, I extend my heartfelt gratitude to my wife, Carla. Her understanding, patience, and support have served as my guiding light throughout the many months spent writing this book.

This book is as much a testament to these remarkable individuals and organizations as it is a reflection of my own passion for AI. I am humbled to contribute to this incredible journey of discovery and innovation, and I am inspired by the potential it holds for our future.

In sum, to all who have been a part of my journey, directly or indirectly, I extend my sincere thanks. This book is a shared accomplishment that I proudly dedicate to all of you.

About the Author

Harish Pursnani is a seasoned technology executive with a 25-year career dedicated to bridging the gap between technology and its users. His innovative mindset, shaped by his advanced studies in Engineering and Computer Science and further honed during his Executive Education at Stanford University Graduate School of Business, has consistently underscored the profound potential of technology to enrich our daily lives.

Throughout a fulfilling career in technology and business transformation, Harish has held prominent roles at esteemed, forward-thinking organizations such as International Business Machines (IBM), PriceWaterhouseCoopers (PwC), and Gilead Sciences Inc. His emphasis on a human-centric approach has allowed him to unlock the genuine value of technology for its users.

More recently, his leadership in digital transformation initiatives has deepened his interest in the transformative potential of Artificial Intelligence. Intrigued by its capability and cognizant of the widening knowledge gap among different societal segments, Harish thoroughly explored the abilities of OpenAI's language model, ChatGPT. His extensive research has culminated in this comprehensive yet accessible guide. Harish aims to distill complex concepts into clear, understandable content, thereby demystifying the pivotal advancement of ChatGPT for readers of diverse backgrounds.

Harish lives in California's Bay Area with his family and an adorable English cream golden retriever. In his personal time, he enjoys spending time with his family, advising startups, trading derivatives, traveling globally, collecting rare stamps, and indulging in continuous learning. This book is an extension of his passion for knowledge, inviting readers from all walks of life to embark on a simplified journey into the transformative world of AI through OpenAI's ChatGPT.

From the Publisher

We trust you have enjoyed and derived value from "ChatGPT Demystified" by Harish Pursnani. Should this book have deepened your understanding of ChatGPT and AI, we kindly request you to share your insights with others by leaving a review on Amazon or the online store from where you made your purchase. Your feedback is not only beneficial to prospective readers but also greatly supports the author.

To explore additional resources and to stay abreast with the latest from Harish Pursnani, we encourage a visit to the book's companion website, **aiunclouded.com**. Here, you will find updates about this book and be privy to other exciting projects.

Anticipate Harish's forthcoming work on Options Trading (expected 2025), backed by his vast experience of over 20 years in trading options and other derivatives. This book is set to provide simplified, insightful, and practical guidance on this complex topic, mirroring the essence of "ChatGPT Demystified".

Beyond Harish Pursnani, we are honored to publish a variety of captivating books from an array of authors. We are particularly excited to showcase D.R. Whimsiquill's collection of children's books, each with a life lesson. To learn more about D.R. Whimsiquill's imaginative and delightful work, please visit **drwhimsiquill.com** or search for the author's name on Amazon, any book retail website, or simply on Google.

As always, our mission is to disseminate knowledge and foster lifelong learning. Thank you for joining us on this journey.